REPORT

T0302505

Chinese Corporate Governance

History and Institutional Framework

Yong Kang, Lu Shi, Elizabeth D. Brown

RAND

Center for Corporate Ethics and Governance

A RAND INSTITUTE FOR CIVIL JUSTICE CENTER

This report results from the RAND Corporation's continuing program of self-initiated research. Support for such research is provided, in part, by the generosity of RAND's donors and by the fees earned on client-funded research. This research was conducted within the RAND Center for Corporate Ethics and Governance, which is part of the RAND Institute for Civil Justice, a unit of the RAND Corporation.

Library of Congress Cataloging-in-Publication Data

Kang, Yong, 1975-
Chinese corporate governance : history and institutional framework / Yong Kang, Lu Shi, Elizabeth D. Brown.
p. cm.
Includes bibliographical references.
ISBN 978-0-8330-4611-6 (pbk. : alk. paper)
1. Corporate governance—China. I. Shi, Lu. II. Brown, Elizabeth D., 1970– III. Title.

HD2741.K36 2008
338.60951—dc22

2008045339

Published 2008 by the RAND Corporation
1776 Main Street, P.O. Box 2138, Santa Monica, CA 90407-2138
1200 South Hayes Street, Arlington, VA 22202-5050
4570 Fifth Avenue, Suite 600, Pittsburgh, PA 15213-2665
RAND URL: http://www.rand.org/
To order RAND documents or to obtain additional information, contact
Distribution Services: Telephone: (310) 451-7002;
Fax: (310) 451-6915; Email: order@rand.org

Preface

The recent history of economic reforms and corporate governance in China has been one of staggeringly swift change, as that nation has moved toward a stronger role for private enterprise and capitalism. As China has aligned itself more closely with the international economy, it has also sought to adopt more Western-style oversight mechanisms and legal standards concerning the operation of its corporations. This report offers a literature review and analysis of the evolution of corporate governance institutions in China, as well as an examination of continuing challenges and policy implications. This report should be of interest to anyone concerned with Chinese corporations, capital markets, securities regulation, or governance issues.

This report results from the RAND Corporation's continuing program of self-initiated research. Support for such research is provided, in part, by the generosity of RAND's donors and by the fees earned on client-funded research.

The RAND Center for Corporate Ethics and Governance

This research was conducted within the RAND Center for Corporate Ethics and Governance, which is part of the RAND Institute for Civil Justice. The Center is committed to improving public understanding of corporate ethics, law, and governance, and to identifying specific ways that businesses can operate ethically, legally, and profitably at the same time. The Center's work is supported by voluntary contributions from private-sector organizations and individuals with interests in research on these topics, and government grants and contracts.

The RAND Institute for Civil Justice (ICJ) is dedicated to improving decisionmaking on civil legal issues by supplying policymakers with the results of objective, empirically based, analytic research. The ICJ facilitates change in the civil justice system by analyzing trends and outcomes, identifying and evaluating policy options, and bringing together representatives of different interests to debate alternative solutions to policy problems. ICJ builds on a long tradition of RAND research characterized by an interdisciplinary, empirical approach to public policy issues and rigorous standards of quality, objectivity, and independence.

ICJ research is supported by pooled grants from corporations, trade and professional associations, and individuals; by government grants and contracts; and by private foundations. ICJ disseminates its work widely to the legal, business, and research communities and to the general public. In accordance with RAND policy, all ICJ research products are subject to peer review before publication. ICJ publications do not necessarily reflect the opinions or policies of the research sponsors or of the ICJ Board of Overseers.

Robert T. Reville, Director
RAND Institute for Civil Justice
1776 Main Street, P.O. Box 2138
Santa Monica, CA 90407–2138
(310) 393–0411 x6786
FAX: (310) 451–6979
Email: Robert_Reville@rand.org

Michael D. Greenberg, Research Director
RAND Center for Corporate Ethics and Governance
4570 Fifth Avenue, Suite 600
Pittsburgh, PA 15213-2665
(412) 682-2300 x4648
FAX: (412) 682-2800
Email: Michael_Greenberg@rand.org

Contents

Figures and Tables

Figures

Tables

Summary

Introduction

Since China started its economic reform in the late 1970s, its gross domestic product has been growing at an average annual rate of 9.73 percent. Chinese stock markets have also been growing rapidly, especially since late 2005, when share merger reform started. Today, there are more than 1,500 publicly traded Chinese companies, and the total market capitalization surpassed 24.5 trillion renminbi (RMB) in August 2007.

Despite this rapid growth, corporate governance has been very weak in China. In a survey by the World Economic Forum, China ranked 44 out of 49 studied countries in terms of corporate governance (Liu, 2006). Corporate governance is critically important to a country's economic growth and stability, because it provides the credibility and confidence in management that is fundamental to capital markets.

To date, research on Chinese corporate governance has been sparse. This report begins to address this gap by providing a basic overview of the status of corporate governance mechanisms in China.

Development of Corporate Governance in China

The historical development of corporate governance in China has gone through four stages. In the first stage, from 1949 to 1983, state-owned enterprises (SOEs) dominated the Chinese economy, and the state commanded and controlled almost every aspect of the economy. Western-style corporate governance did not exist in China.

The second stage, from 1984 to 1993, involved the beginning of the separation of government and enterprise in China. During this period, China formally established the Shanghai Stock Exchange (SSE) and the Shenzhen Stock Exchange (SZSE), and a new government body, the China Securities Regulatory Commission (CSRC), was created to be the country's main regulator of the newborn stock market.

The third stage, from 1994 to 2005, marked the beginning of experimentation in modern enterprise structure, including passage of the first Company Law—the first comprehensive law that fully delineated the rights and responsibilities for modern companies in China. Although the Company Law has had a far-reaching impact on corporate governance and the economy as a whole in China, state shareholders still enjoyed overwhelming favoritism over individual investors.

The final stage, from 2006 onward, has witnessed the continuing growth of corporate governance in China, including legislation aimed at balancing the power asymmetry between state shareholders and individual shareholders in companies.

The Institutional Framework

Many entities both inside and outside companies play a role in shaping the behavior and governance of Chinese companies. The inner circle of oversight consists of shareholders' general meetings, boards, and management personnel who are engaged in operating the companies and are directly responsible for their governance. The outer circle is composed of regulators (chiefly, the CSRC), stock exchanges (the SSE and SZSE), the Chinese legal system, the auditing system, and institutional investors. These players have a significant impact on companies' corporate governance, but they mainly do this through regulation, codes of conduct, certification of financial reports, and legal enforcement. Besides these institutional pillars, there are other agents who may also affect corporate governance (e.g., consumers, suppliers, employees, media, and nongovernmental organizations).

Problems of Corporate Governance in China

Despite recent reforms made in corporate governance controls and institutions in China, a number of problems still remain. First, there is **concentration of state ownership.** Approximately two-thirds of companies listed in the SSE are state enterprises, which leads to inefficiency in capital allocation, whether it comes directly from a government body or through a brokerage firm.

Second, a direct result of ownership concentration is the **lack of independence among board directors**. Given the overwhelming governmental dominance of Chinese boards of directors, the supervisory board in China has not yet played a significant and effective governance role.

Third, **insider trading** is a very serious problem among China's listed companies. Reasons for this include the lack of a well-defined concept for fiduciary duty, inefficient enforcement of securities laws, the absence of class actions in China, and the lack of any incentive mechanism to encourage reporting or whistle-blowing about insider trading.

Fourth, **false financial disclosures** by companies remain a significant problem. According to a random check by the Ministry of Finance, a significant number of Chinese companies forged their earnings in annual reports in 2001.

Finally, China continues to suffer from **immature capital markets**, characterized by the Chinese banks' preferential treatment of SOEs, difficulties in issuing corporate bonds, and the absence of preferred shares as a financing/investment option.

Conclusion

China has made rapid progress in corporate governance, in part because of the gradual removal of ownership and personnel barriers, coupled with an increasingly globalized and mature business environment. However, despite this rapid progress, serious problems abound in various aspects of Chinese corporate governance, ranging from company ownership structures to the media environment in which Chinese companies and security markets operate.

Several options have been proposed to deal with these problems, including more clearly defining the functions of the supervisory boards, making it easier for whistleblowers to sue management, toughening legal obligations for managers involved in insider trading, lowering the minimum required number of shares for shareholders to raise proposals, increasing the legal obligation of controlling shareholders, and developing a long-term focus incentive compensation system for directors and executives (e.g., long-term nontradable options).

In addition, we propose reviving and institutionalizing the once-banned, regional, over-the-counter markets, because doing so would offer an opportunity to improve the corporate governance of Chinese enterprises, while providing a buffer zone for companies facing the risk of delisting in the stock exchanges. Similarly, accelerating the development of the corporate debt market could help meet the needs of the more risk-averse investors and, thereby, increase the capital supply for Chinese companies in need of steady capital input. Finally, we suggest establishing an incentive mechanism to encourage the reporting of insider trading. Increasing the organizational performance of the CSRC and stock exchanges and promulgating the concept of fiduciary duty will take a considerable amount of time and cost. By contrast, providing incentives for exposing insider trading would likely cost less and could be more effective as a governance mechanism in China than in the United States.

Acknowledgments

We want to thank Robert T. Reville, William H. Overholt, C. Richard Neu, and Michael D. Greenberg for their helpful comments and support during the course of the study. We are also grateful for helpful discussions with participants at the RAND Center for Corporate Ethics and Governance Advisory Meeting in New York, which was held from May 15 to 17, 2007. William Overholt and Anthea Zhang's insightful and constructive reviews helped us greatly in improving the original draft. We really appreciate their efforts. Needlessly to say, any errors remain ours.

Abbreviations

ASBE	Accounting Standards for Business Enterprises
CICPA	Chinese Institute of Certified Public Accountants
CNAO	Chinese National Accounting Office
CPA	certified public accountant
CSRC	China Securities Regulatory Commission
GDP	gross domestic product
IPO	initial public offering
MOF	Ministry of Finance (Chinese)
NGO	nongovernmental organization
OECD	Organisation for Economic Co-operation and Development
OTC	over-the-counter
P/E	price-earnings (ratio)
QFII	Qualified Foreign Institutional Investor
RMB	renminbi (Chinese yuan)
SCSC	State Council's Securities Commission (Chinese)
SEC	U.S. Securities and Exchange Commission
SOE	state-owned enterprise
SPC	Supreme People's Court of China
SSE	Shanghai Stock Exchange
SZSE	Shenzhen Stock Exchange
WTO	World Trade Organization

CHAPTER ONE

Introduction

Corporate governance is critically important to a country's economic growth and stability, because it provides the credibility and confidence that is fundamental to capital markets (Organisation for Economic Co-operation and Development [OECD], 2004; Centre for Financial Market Integrity, 2007). Companies that are perceived to have better corporate governance receive more trust from investors and usually enjoy a lower cost of capital and higher market valuation than others (Bai et al., 2004). The highly publicized corporate scandals that involved once-prestigious U.S. companies, such as Enron and WorldCom, highlight the urgent need to strengthen corporate governance institutions. In addition, companies can now draw financing from a much larger pool of global investors as the world economy is becoming more interlinked, but this also implies that the corporate governance of companies in one country may have a far-reaching impact on other economies. For example, even though inappropriate macroeconomic policies during the 1990s were considered an important reason for the 1997–1998 Asian financial crisis, poor corporate governance greatly deepened the extent of the negative impacts (Johnson et al., 2000). As a result, the International Monetary Fund explicitly required the affected countries to improve their corporate governance as a condition of its debt relief program.

Although corporate governance has received increasing recent attention from both scholars and the public, there still lacks a uniform, widely accepted definition of the subject. Classical research focuses on the separation of ownership and management, and thus views corporate governance as a set of systems and rules by which companies are run (Megginson and Netter, 2001; Skousen, Glover, and Prawitt, 2005). For example, Adrian Cadbury, the former head of the Committee on the Financial Aspects of Corporate Governance in the United Kingdom, states that "Corporate governance is the system by which companies are directed and controlled" (Cadbury Report, 1992).

This definition, however, leaves unanswered an important question regarding how a company should be run. There are two major schools of thought on this issue. One, sometimes called "shareholder theory," asserts that the primary goal of corporate governance should be to protect investors against expropriation by management. For example, in a survey of research on corporate governance, Shleifer and Vishny (1997) define "corporate governance" as dealing with "the ways in which suppliers of finance to corporations assure themselves of getting a return on their investment" (p. 737). The other approach is often referred to as "stakeholder theory." It treats corporate governance in a broader context, and asserts that corporate governance should consider not only investors' interests, but also the interests of other stakeholders, such as employees, customers, suppliers, and communities, who might be affected directly or indirectly by companies' behaviors (Charreaux and Desbrieres, 2001).

There are still many debates on which approach provides the best way to study corporate governance. Each approach has its advantages and shortcomings. Shareholder theory is based on extensively researched principal-agency relationships and develops a set of well-defined incentive and control mechanisms, but the theory has been challenged by social activists as failing to recognize the broader impact of company behavior. Stakeholder theory, by contrast, encourages companies to internalize benefits and costs on society and take more social responsibility, but this theory offers less insight regarding how the interest of management can be effectively aligned with that of a group of diversified shareholders (Tirole, 2001).

While it is beyond the scope of this paper to discuss these two approaches in detail, we focus on the protection of investors' interest in our study of corporate governance in China. As China is transiting from a centrally planned to a market-based economy, privatizing state enterprises and granting property rights to individuals have been the key elements of economic reform. Prior to the early 1980s, individuals used to have no real ownership in state enterprises, and their compensations were not linked with companies' performance. As a product of reforms, especially after the establishment of Chinese capital markets, individuals are gradually gaining property rights and becoming investors in companies. However, China is still working to build up its market economy, and individual investors' interest is poorly guarded and often expropriated by controlling shareholders and management. Therefore, it is not surprising that a central theme of past research on corporate governance in China has been the protection of investor interest. For example, a prominent Chinese economist defines corporate governance as the relationship among owners, boards of directors, and management, and stresses the checks and balances on control and incentives (Wu, 1994). We follow this path in our own research, and focus on the role of corporate governance in protecting investors' interest, especially that of non-controlling shareholders.

Academic research on corporate governance can be traced back to Adam Smith. He argued that managers of joint-stock companies might not watch over the companies as if they were the owners. In a classic work, Berle and Means (1932) show that the separation of ownership and control allows managers to pursue their own interests rather than those of the shareholders. Jensen and Meckling (1976) show that law and contracts are essential to prevent managers from expropriating the investors, and to ensure a healthy capital market. Research on corporate governance has traditionally focused on the United States. However, with the rapid growth of globalization, an increasing amount of research has been done on corporate governance in other countries. For example, the pioneering works of Schleifer and Vishny (1997) and La Porta et al. (1998, 1999, 2000) compare corporate governance in different countries based on their political and judicial systems. But most of the research focuses on developed countries, and studies on corporate governance in developing countries remain sparse. This report is intended to address the gap, by providing an overview of the development and institutional framework for corporate governance in China.

Since China started its economic reform in the late 1970s, its gross domestic product (GDP) has been growing at an average annual rate of 9.73 percent (Figure 1.1).

China had opened its two stock markets, Shanghai Stock Exchange (SSE) and Shenzhen Stock Exchange (SZSE), by the end of 1990.[1] There were only eight issued stocks and the total

[1] Toward the end of 1990, many cities were competing to open their own stock markets. Some of them did so without authorization from the central government. Even to date, there are still some debates between Shanghai Stock Exchange and Shenzhen Stock Exchange as to which was the first stock market in China. In any case, the goal of the Chinese govern-

Figure 1.1
China's Economic Growth

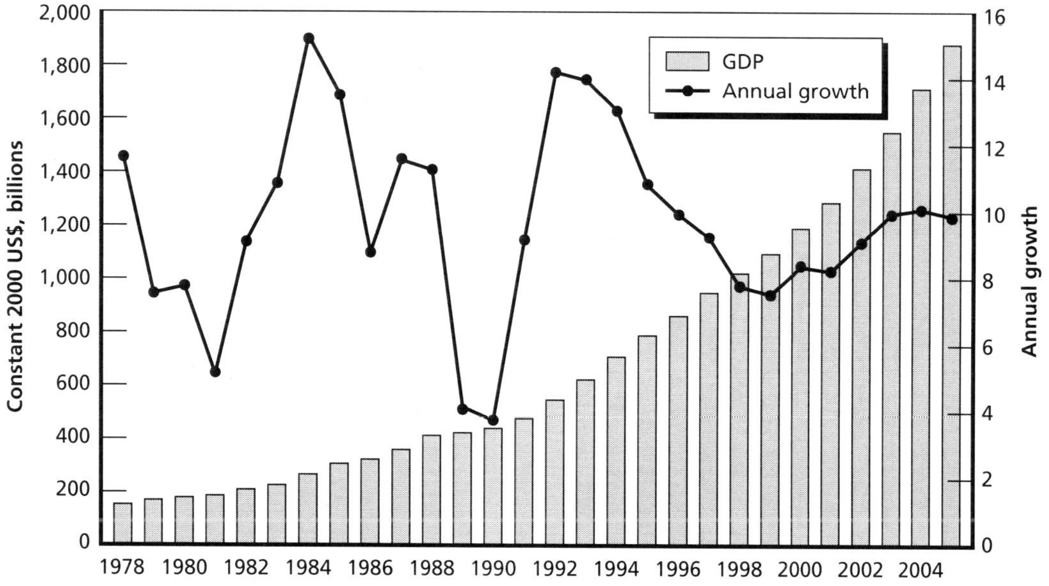

SOURCE: World Development Indicator, the World Bank Group (various years).
RAND *TR618-1.1*

market capitalization was a mere 260 million renminbi (RMB).[2] However, Chinese stock markets have been growing rapidly, especially since late 2005, when the share merger reform (*gu quan fen zhi gai ge*) started. This reform will gradually release previously nontradable shares into the market and help improve the liquidity of the Chinese capital markets (a detailed discussion on share merger reform can be found in Chapter Two). Today there are more than 1,500 publicly traded companies in China, and the total market capitalization surpassed 24.5 trillion (RMB) in August 2007.[3]

Nonetheless, corporate governance has remained very weak in China. According to a survey by the World Economic Forum, China ranked 44 out of 49 studied countries in terms of corporate governance (Liu, 2006; see Table 1.1). Insider control and self-dealing are so rampant in China that a famous Chinese economist once called the stock markets "a casino without rules."[4]

With China's accession to the World Trade Organization in 2001, its economy has become more integrated into the world economy. As a result, understanding corporate governance institutions that affect Chinese companies is increasingly important.

---

ment was not to build up Western-style corporate governance or accelerate economic development, but instead to recapitalize major state enterprises. We thank William Overholt for pointing this out to us.

[2] "Lao Ba Gu: Cheng Tou Bian Huan Da Wang Qi" (2005).

[3] China's stock markets have dropped dramatically since October 2007. Many factors contribute to the tumble, including the uncertainty of the impact of the U.S. subprime mortgage crisis on China, soaring global commodities prices, and rising inflationary pressure and the influx of formerly nontradable shares into the market.

[4] "Wu Jing Lian Nu Chi Gu Shi Hei Zhuang" (2001).

Table 1.1
Ranking of Corporate Governance Around the World (2003)

Rank	Country	Score
1	United Kingdom	6.34
6	Sweden	5.98
7	United States	5.94
8	Singapore	5.91
9	Germany	5.78
13	Hong Kong	5.59
23	Taiwan	4.96
28	Thailand	4.72
31	Japan	4.59
32	India	4.59
33	Korea	4.59
43	Philippines	3.89
44	**China**	**3.80**
46	Indonesia	3.62

SOURCE: Liu (2006).

This report aims to provide a basic understanding of corporate governance mechanisms in China, and to identify areas for future research. Chapter Two divides the historical development of corporate governance in China into four stages, and reviews the background and distinct features of corporate governance in each stage. Chapter Three further investigates corporate governance from the perspective of institutional framework, and discusses eight institutional pillars that are essential to the structure of corporate governance in China. In Chapter Four, we turn to a discussion of the current problems associated with corporate governance in China. Chapter Five concludes with policy implications and a future research agenda.

CHAPTER TWO

The Development of Corporate Governance in China

1949–1983: Dominance of State-Owned Enterprises

During the pre-reform era from 1949 to 1979, the vast majority of corporate citizens in the Chinese economy were state-owned enterprises (SOEs), economic entities that were owned and operated by the government. The whole economy of the state sector was organized into one giant corporation, in which the state controlled everything from manufacturing to distribution and consumption (Wu, 1994). The party secretary's job in an SOE was to coordinate and supervise workers and to implement the production plan created by the central and local governments. The entire workforce was paid through a national wage hierarchy, which was modeled after the payment structure of government employees. In addition, local governments were allowed to establish small enterprises that were jointly owned by local communities rather than the Chinese state (collectively owned enterprises), in which the employees received considerably fewer benefits than did their counterparts in state-owned enterprises. Private ownership of any enterprise was strictly prohibited. Similar to communist economies across the world, the Chinese governance structure incurred considerable resource-allocation inefficiency.

Family businesses emerged during the early and mid-1970s in some parts of China, despite their illegal status (Watts, 2005). Not long after Deng Xiaoping's accession to power in 1978, the state recognized the legitimacy of these private enterprises, and the entrepreneurs in turn obtained licenses for their business operations (Wang et al., 2003). Although the emerging private sector marked a diversification of ownership in the Chinese corporate world, the country's economy in the 1980s continued to be dominated by SOEs (Figure 2.1). During this period, the state not only was the owner of all the enterprises, but also commanded and controlled almost every aspect of the economy. Western-style corporate governance did not exist in China at this time.

1984–1993: Separation of Government and Enterprise

In October 1984, the Communist Party's central committee announced the decisions of the Central Committee on Economic Structural Reform, marking the beginning of enterprise reform. For the first time, this committee explicitly ordered the separation of government intervention from enterprise operation. The goal was to transform firms into economic entities that could make their own decisions and be held responsible for their own profits or losses, thus creating a more effective incentive scheme among Chinese companies. The reform was

Figure 2.1
China's Industrial Output, by Ownership, in 1985

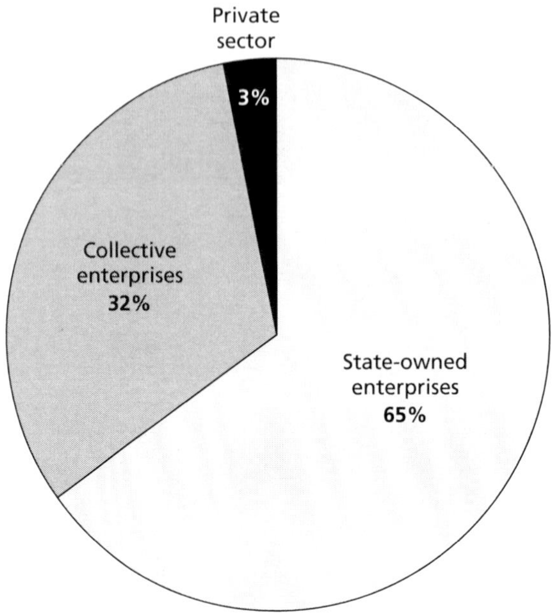

SOURCE: National Bureau of Statistics of the People's Republic of China (2008).
RAND *TR618-2.1*

not intended to change the state's ownership, but rather to remedy the inefficiency of SOEs (Zhang, 1998).

The implementation of the 1984 reform initiatives started with the policy of granting autonomy to companies and allowing them to retain a certain portion of profit, and was soon followed by the management contract system in the mid-1980s. The State Council's "Decisions on Deepening Enterprise Reform and Invigorating Enterprises," announced in December 1986, sped up the reform and made it the norm among SOEs by 1989 (Yuan and Zhang, 2003). A typical management contract delineates profit-sharing rules through negotiations between a management team and related governmental agencies. Under such a contract, the firm typically retains extra profit after fulfilling the fixed remittance target, often with its total wage system linked to the actual profit and tax. These contracts led to a steady increase in marginal profit retention rates over the 1980s (Groves et al., 1994). Taken together with price deregulation in commodity and factor markets, as well as a reduction in directive production plans, SOE managers in China have gradually obtained considerable freedom in management practice.

In August 1984, the Shanghai Municipal Government approved the first provincial-level regulation on securities, which marked the beginning of the stockholding system of Chinese enterprises. Three months later, a household electronics company issued the first stock in post-1949 China. That stock became tradable over-the-counter in 1986 (Ellman, 1988). During the latter half of the 1980s, more and more SOEs followed the path of securitization. As a result, China formally established the SSE and the SZSE in 1990. The following year, a new government body, the China Securities Regulatory Commission (CSRC), was created to serve as the country's main regulator of the newborn stock market. Circulated in these two stock markets were two types of shares: A shares and B shares. The former refers to the stocks valued in RMB and available only to Chinese citizens; the latter are denominated in RMB but traded in such foreign currencies as the U.S. dollar or the Hong Kong dollar. Until 2001, B shares were restricted to foreign citizens and residents of Hong Kong, Taiwan, and Macao. Newly listed companies usually had sold shares to their employees prior to initial public offerings (IPOs); the establishment of the two stock exchanges was expected to provide SOE employees with a stronger incentive to buy shares.

Although these reforms brought about stronger incentives for SOE managers to increase profits, the reforms were not without limitations. Notably, government agencies sometimes selected managers from within a key bureaucrat's social network or replaced the management team with cronies once an SOE began to make impressive profit, both detrimental for improving SOEs' financial performance. Managers of SOEs made investments in quick revenue-generating projects—rather than investing in long-term productivity-enhancing projects and research and development—because of the short-term nature of their management contracts with the state (Huang et al., 1998). A gloomy indicator of the insufficiency of merely corporatizing SOEs without fully reforming their ownership structure was the debt-to-asset ratio of the whole industrial SOEs sector, which increased from 18.7 percent in 1980 to about 67.9 percent in 1994 (Wu and Xie, 1997). The SOE debt issue became a major threat to China's economic survivability in the mid-1990s and served as a strong motivation for further ownership reform.

1994–2005: Experimentation in the Modern Enterprise Structure

The Standing Committee of the People's Congress issued China's first Company Law in December 1993, defining the maximization of owners' interests as the primary goal of corporate practice. It was the first comprehensive law that fully delineated the rights and responsibilities of modern companies in China. More importantly, it was the first major business law in China that did not differentiate legislation for companies based on their ownership structures. In the past, Chinese enterprise laws had been enacted according to the type of ownership: Several examples are the Sino-Foreign Joint Enterprises Law (1979), Foreign Companies Law (1986), SOEs Law (1988), Temporary Regulations of Privately Owned Enterprises (1988), and Rules for Rural Collectively Owned Enterprises (1990). Instead, the 1993 Company Law classified companies into two groups, limited liability companies and joint stock limited liability companies, based on the size of shareholders. This law was regarded a major step toward the modernization of Chinese legislation (Wang and Cui, 2006).

The Company Law has had far-reaching impact on corporate governance and the economy as a whole in China. In 1994, the slogan, "corporatization of SOEs," which meant increasing private ownership in former SOEs, replaced the once-popular management contract system, even though the actual process of SOE corporatization had begun about 10 years earlier. As of 1996, approximately 5,800 industrial SOEs had been corporatized, and a number of them had made their initial public offerings in China's nascent stock exchanges, which were established in 1991 (World Bank, 1997). The fact that SOE managers typically owned nontradable shares of these listed SOEs indicated that a process of implicit privatization had already begun to take place, even though the word "privatization" remained more or less a political taboo in the early

1990s. As a result, managers had a much stronger incentive than before to produce authentic profits, because it affected their own wealth accumulation.

Though the reform actions in the early and mid-1990s might look revolutionary in a communist country, the Chinese economic system still suffered from overwhelming favoritism toward the SOEs. The SOEs continued to enjoy favorable treatment from the initial process of company establishment all the way through to public offerings of securities, and they therefore continued to survive even after the enactment of the 1993 Company Law. The state was confused between its role as a regulator and social planner aimed at maximizing the aggregate social welfare, versus its role as an investor aimed at maximizing shareholder profit. Nonstate institutional investors and individual investors, confined by their lack of power in governance as well as insufficient legal protection, usually ended up engaged in speculative behavior rather than investment behavior. An average Chinese investor owned his or her shares for less than four months, compared with the U.S. average of 17 months (Chen et al., 2005; Zhou, 2005). The CSRC made numerous efforts to address the lack of checks and balances among listed companies. Faced with powerful political entities as owners of listed companies, the real impacts of its efforts were often limited. The 1998 Securities Law, passed partly in response to the Asian financial crisis, allowed investors to sue management and directors for releasing false or misleading company information, but these rights were rarely exercised to protect investors' interest (Ho, 2003).

After the passage of the 1998 Securities Law, the power of the CSRC was significantly strengthened and it took a more active role in monitoring and regulating corporate governance of public companies. For example, the CSRC published guidelines for introducing independent directors to the Board of Directors in listed companies in August 2001. The CSRC stipulated that at least one-third of trustee board members of all publicly listed companies should be independent directors. In January 2002, the CSRC and the State Economic and Trade Commission jointly issued Code of Corporate Governance for Listed Companies, the first of such code in China. The code paid special attention to the protection of shareholders' investors, especially small investors, and prohibited controlling shareholders from expropriating the minority shareholders.

The real effect of independent directors on corporate governance was questionable. Most of the independent directors had no stake in the performance of the company and therefore lacked incentives to influence corporate governance. Nor were they powerful enough to reverse companywide decisionmaking that could harm minor shareholders' interest. For example, in 2004 the country's dairy giant, the Yili Group, removed an independent director from the board after the director demanded an independent auditing of the company's investment in government bonds, a program that aroused the suspicion of several independent directors (Yu, 2004). It seemed, therefore, that the real solution for the power and information asymmetry between the dominant owner (the state) and minority investors could only be found with further ownership reform, which the government resumed in 2005.

2006 Onward: Continued Pursuit of Corporate Governance

Until 2005, about two-thirds of the stocks in China's security markets were nontradable. They included both the state-owned shares and legal-person shares that are owned by employees and parent companies. These nontradable shares constituted a significant and persistent risk for minority investors in tradable shares, because no law protected their interests in the case of floating nontradable shares. Accompanying the efforts to achieve information symmetry between minor shareholders and the major shareholders, the Chinese government initiated a program to fully circulate listed companies' nontradable shares. Listed companies were required to circulate their nontradable shares, with a compensation package approved by the holders of tradable shares. Listed companies that underwent this process were shown to perform significantly better in the stock market than those that did not, which implies that circulating state-owned shares of listed companies helped gain investors' confidence and thus opened a door for improving China's corporate governance in general.

In October 2005, the National People's Congress passed a revision of China's Company Law, which turned the 2002 CSRC requirement of independent directors into a legal necessity. The revision also required that board directors abstain from voting on issues that were related to their own interest. Under the new Company Law, shareholders were entitled to appeal to the supervisory board to resolve what they deemed as misconduct by the managers and board directors, and they were entitled to appeal to the board of directors to resolve what they deemed as the misconduct by members of the supervisory board. The new law also entitled shareholders to appeal to the court to start a bankruptcy process, provided that the decision was supported by at least 10 percent of shareholder votes. Finally, shareholders were granted the right to demand a buyback of shares under certain conditions when shareholder interests might suffer.

The 2005 version of the Company Law also lowered the threshold for companies' public listing. For example, before the law's enactment in October 2005, companies that wanted to undertake an IPO had to obtain official approval from the State Council, whereas the new company law removed this requirement. For start-up enterprises, the 2005 Company Law lowered the required capital registration from 100,000 yuan to 50,000 yuan. Other significant changes in this legislation included the recognition of intellectual property and stock as forms of capital investment and the removal of the requirement that a limited liability company be established by more than one shareholder. All in all, these amendments marked a decisive step toward encouraging entrepreneurship and minority shareholder rights. A similar perspective on the 2005 Company Law was expressed by commentators in the *WTO Tribune*:

> The general provisions of the amended law require that the company must abide by the law and administrative regulations, comply with social ethics, business ethics, honesty and trustworthiness, accept the supervision of the government and the general public and bear the social responsibility. It is the first time that Company Law clearly put forward that enterprises should shoulder their social responsibilities. We believe that it will play a significant role in promoting China's corporate social responsibility. (Yin and Wu, 2007)

In 2006, the National People's Congress amended the 1998 Securities Law, with the similar goal of balancing the power asymmetry between the state owner and the minority shareholders. Similar to the milestone of deregulating listed companies' investment activities, the new Securities Law lifted the ban that kept public listed companies from entering new industries. This granted corporations the right to freely enter industries that they deemed worthy of their investment. The amended version of the Securities Law also opened the door for methods of trading shares other than spot trading.

On the front of protecting investor interests, the new Securities Law required that an investor protection fund be established with financing from investment banks. The amendments specified that funds derived from the settlement of transactions of investors be deposited in commercial banks, prohibiting investment banks from manipulating these investor funds or securities as part of their own funds.

As Chinese lawmakers worked to close the corporate governance gap between China and developed nations, China's executive branch also moved ahead in protecting minority shareholders. Shenzhen Stock Exchange, for example, began building up a market surveillance system that closely monitors share price fluctuations to prevent illegal stock manipulation. It also suspended or delisted 102 companies in 2006, primarily for failing to improve information transparency, reflecting a sharp increase in enforcement activity from previous years. Shenzhen Stock Exchange also took measures to forcibly disclose information pertinent to investors' interest that public companies chose not to announce. All of these initiatives improved investors' confidence and helped foster the stock market rally after 2005.

CHAPTER THREE

The Institutional Framework

In order to gain a proper understanding of how corporate governance works in China, it is essential to become familiar with the institutional framework. There are many entities that play an important role in shaping companies' behaviors in China. They can be roughly divided into two main groups: those operating inside the company, and those operating outside the company (Figure 3.1). The inner circle consists of the shareholders' general meeting, boards, and management. All three are engaged in the operation of the company and are directly responsible for its governance. The outer circle is composed of regulators (chiefly the CSRC), stock exchanges (SSE and SZSE), the legal system, the auditing system, and institutional investors. These external players have a significant impact on a company's corporate governance, but they mainly do this through regulations, codes of conducts, certification of financial reports, legal enforcement, etc. Besides these institutional pillars, there are other agents that may also affect corporate governance, for example, consumers, suppliers, employees, media, and nongovernmental organizations (NGOs). In this chapter, we investigate each of these players to generate a broad list of corporate governance issues and stakeholders in China.

Shareholders' General Meeting

The Company Law empowers the general meeting of shareholders to be the ultimate decisionmaking entity for a corporation. According to Article 101 of the Company Law, the general meeting of shareholders is required to be held once a year except under the following special circumstances, when a temporary meeting must be called within two months:

- when the number of board directors is fewer than two thirds required by law or the company by-law
- when the uncompensated losses of the company exceed one-third of the actual capital
- at the request of the shareholders separately or collectively holding 10 percent or more of the company's shares
- when deemed necessary by the board of directors or supervisory board
- in other situations specified by the company by-law.

A shareholders' general meeting is convened and presided over by the chair of the board of directors. The board of directors is responsible for the meeting agenda. Article 103 of the Company Law specified that shareholders separately or in aggregate holding 3 percent or more of the company shares can submit a written proposal to the board of directors at least 10 days

Figure 3.1
Institutional Players Related to Corporate Governance in China

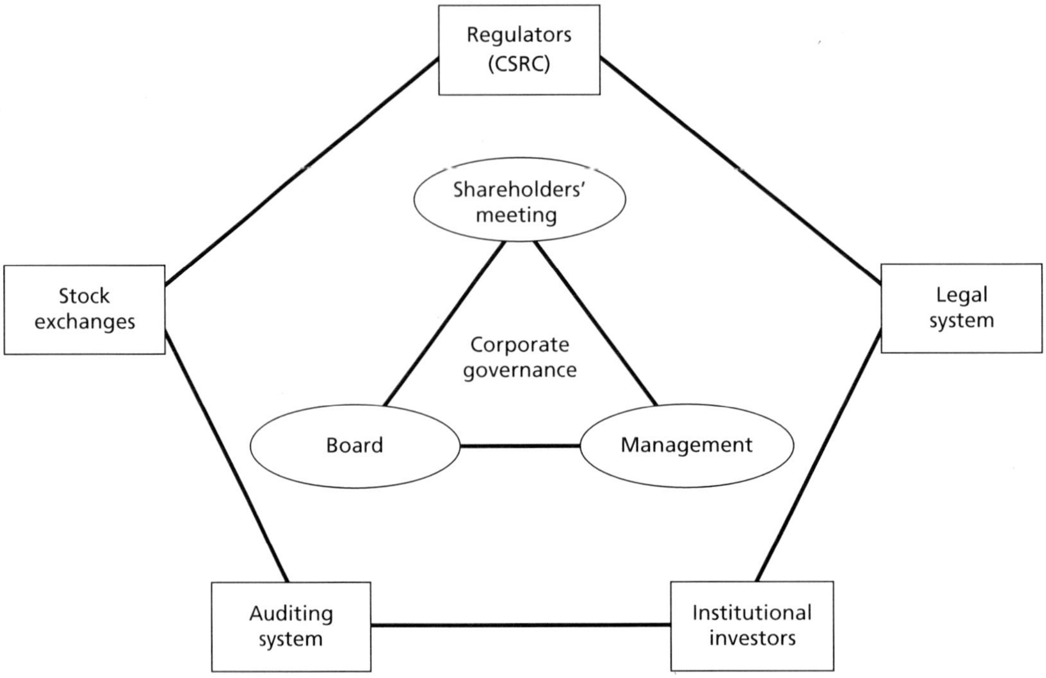

RAND *TR618-3.1*

before the general meeting, to add issues to the agenda to be discussed. However, some commentators have suggested that the threshold is too high for small and medium investors to make their voices heard in the shareholders' meeting (Ning, 2006).

Article 104 of the Company Law states that the general decision rule of the meeting is one-share, one-vote. In order to be adopted, a resolution has to win at least half of the voting rights in the presence of the meeting. For important issues, such as modifying company's by-laws, mergers and acquisitions, and divestitures, a supermajority of two-thirds of the voting rights is required.

A major revision in the 2005 Company Law (Article 106) permits a company to adopt a cumulative voting system during the shareholders' meeting, in selecting board directors and supervisors. According to the cumulative voting system, each share has the right of voting equal to the number of candidates to be elected, and a shareholder can cast all his/her votes on one candidate. This new rule is particularly important in China, where a single shareholder or several large shareholders can often control a dominant amount of shares. It gives small and medium investors relatively more strength in selecting the board. To illustrate, consider a company with 100 shares and 10 shareholders. One shareholder takes absolute control with 51 percent of the shares, and the remaining shareholders collectively own 49 percent. The shareholders' meeting is to elect five board directors. In the absence of a cumulative voting system, the controlling shareholder can make sure all his candidates are elected. However, in the cumulative voting system, the total votes become 100 × 5 = 500; the controlling shareholder has 255 votes (500 × 51), while the other shareholders are equipped with 245 votes (500 × 49 percent). Since the first five candidates with the most votes will be elected, the non-controlling shareholders can, in theory, ensure at least two of their board directors will be elected.

Another major revision of the 2005 Company Law deals with proxy voting. Under Article 107 of the law, shareholders now can entrust proxies to attend the general meeting and exercise their voting rights under authorization. Proxy voting can help dispersed minority investors to act collectively, and to have their voices heard. However, the law doesn't specify how proxy voting should be implemented and monitored.

Attendance at general meetings of shareholders in China has usually been very low, and dominated by the controlling shareholders. From 2000 to 2002, the average number of shareholders attending the general meeting decreased (see Figure 3.2; *People's Daily*, 2004). Most individual shareholders chose not to attend the general meetings because they feel their votes have very limited influence on companies' decisions and that the high costs in transportation and time are not justified.

Board

Listed companies in China have a two-tier board, with separate boards of directors and boards of supervisors. Table 3.1 compares the differences and similarities between these two boards.

The two-tier board structure in China in appearance resembles the German model, where the management board makes decisions on day-to-day operations and the supervisory board overseas the management board and approves major business decisions. Despite the appearance, however, the Chinese system is actually more similar to the one-tier board in the United States. The supervisory board in China is notably much smaller than in the German board. Supervisory boards in China do not have authority to select or dismiss board directors or management, and they often lack the knowledge and experience to effectively supervise the direc-

Figure 3.2
Attendance of Shareholders' General Meeting

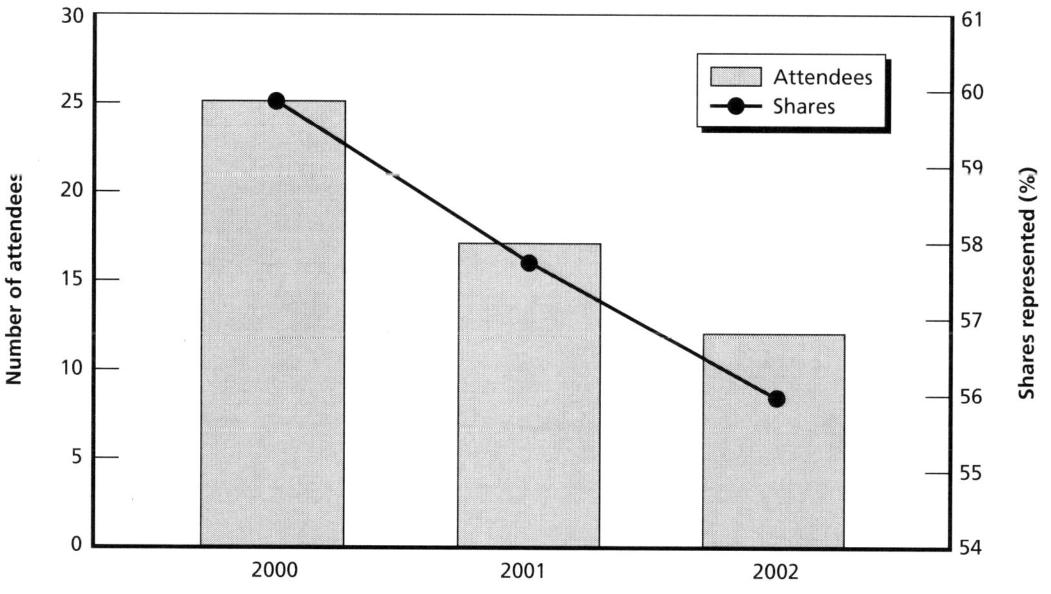

SOURCE: *People's Daily* (2004).
RAND *TR618-3.2*

Table 3.1
Comparison of the Board of Directors and Board of Supervisors

	Board of Directors	Board of Supervisors
Size	5–19	At least 3
Length of each term	3 years	3 years
Renewable	Yes	Yes
Employee representative	No requirement	At least one-third
Main responsibility	Convene the general meeting of shareholders and prepare meeting agendas; vote on important issues related to company operation; make decisions on stock issuing, mergers and acquisitions, spin-offs, significant investments; recruit and dismiss senior management and decide their compensations	Monitor the board of directors and senior management; call up temporary shareholders' meeting if the board of directors fails to do so
Meeting frequency	At least twice a year	At least once every 6 months
Eligibility of management to be a member	Yes	No

tors and management. These difficulties make the monitoring role of the supervisory board weak and (arguably) illusory (Schipani and Liu, 2001; Ho, 2003). Some surveys also show that the quasi-two-tier board can lead to redundancy and inefficiency in corporate governance (Institute of International Finance, 2006; Centre for Financial Market Integrity, 2007).

The board of directors is the de facto decisionmaking authority, and the chairman of the board is normally the most powerful person in all company decisions. The chair often surpasses the chief executive officer (CEO) and other senior executives to engage in daily management (Di, Ren, and Wang, 2005).

Both the Code on Corporate Governance for Listed Companies (2002) and the Company Law (2003) explicitly stress the duty of loyalty and diligence of the directors to shareholders. If a director violates the law, a regulation, or the company's by-laws and jeopardizes shareholders' interest, shareholders can sue the director in court and ask for compensation (Article 153 of the Company Law). However, the monitoring role of boards of directors is questionable, as they are often dominated by representatives from parent companies, and/or by party secretaries or government officials. The quality of the board is also low (Ho, 2003). Chen, Fan, and Wong (2003) studied the boards of directors of 621 companies from 1993 to 2000 and found that about 52 percent of the directors were former or current employees of the largest shareholders, and that roughly 32 percent were current or former government bureaucrats. Directors with professional backgrounds, such as in law, accounting, and finance, are rare, accounting for only 5 percent of board members on average.

In August 2001, the CSRC promulgated the guidelines for introducing independent directors to the boards of directors in listed companies. It required that listed companies have at least one-third of their boards consist of independent directors by June 2003. However, qualified independent directors were a scarce resource in China. By May 2003, it was reported that only 62 percent of listed companies met this requirement (Green, 2004). The proportion of independent directors has significantly increased since then, but it remains doubtful how well they represent the interest of minority shareholders and how much influence they may have on management and other directors of the board.

Management

Managers of SOEs used to be similar to government bureaucrats in China (Hua, Miesing, and Li, 2006). They were appointed by either state or local governments, and shared the same career path as government officials. The main duty of managers was simply to organize production under the direction of the government. They had no control over the quantity or price of the products that they produced, and it was very difficult for them to fire nonqualified workers. Their compensation was not very different from regular workers.

The central theme of SOE reform since the 1980s has been to increase managers' autonomy and improve their incentive systems (Naughton, 1994). Enterprises are now viewed as economic entities that should be responsible for their own profits or losses. In principle, general managers of SOEs ought to have full authority on how to run their firms, and their compensations should be linked to the firms' performance. In practice, the better-aligned incentive system has helped improve SOEs' efficiencies. Li (1997) estimated that, between 1980 and 1989, over 87 percent of growth in total factor productivity resulted from improved incentives, intensified market competition, and improved factor allocation.

Under Article 114 of the Company Law, a company's senior management is appointed by the board of directors, but the board's decision may be greatly influenced by government intervention in former SOEs. Zhang (1997, 1998) believes that management selection poses the biggest challenge to enterprise reform in China. In fact, the central government often rotates the top jobs of large SOEs in an effort to avoid the development of entrenched interests. For example, in November 2004, Chinese authorities suddenly announced a series of position changes in large telecommunication companies: moving the senior vice president of China Mobile to the top position of China Telcom, appointing the CEO of China Unicom as the chair of China Mobile, and promoting the deputy president of China Telcom to the chair of China Unicom. These dazzling job swaps within the largest Chinese telecommunication companies would be unlikely if the boards were exercising independent authority.

According to a government rule published in November 2003,[1] there are two components in the compensation package of senior managers of large SOEs: a base annual salary and an annual bonus based on company performance. Each year, senior managers are evaluated based on their companies' performance during the specific year and their entire tenures. Then their performance is given a letter ranking, A through E. If a manager's performance ranks an E, he or she would not receive a bonus. Meanwhile, if a manager's performance is ranked an A, the bonus could be up to three times his or her base annual salary.[2] Du (2005) cites a study commissioned by the Development Research Center of the State Council showing that the average salary of top management[3] in SOEs directly controlled by the central government in 2003 was 362,000 RMB (about $44,000). This was about 11.9 times higher than the average salary of a regular employee in the same industry. It is true that the senior management of these companies often receive many non-pecuniary benefits, such as chauffeured cars, free housing, and

---

1 The Temporary Rules on Performance Evaluation of Senior Managers of Enterprises Owned by the Central Government (2003).

2 Temporary Rules on Performance Evaluation of Senior Managers of Enterprises Owned by the Central Government (2003), Article 23.

3 Including chairman of the board, vice chair, president, CEO, chief financial officer (CFO), and other senior-level executives.

Figure 3.3
Salaries of Senior Managers and Regular Employees in SOEs Controlled by the Central Government (2003)

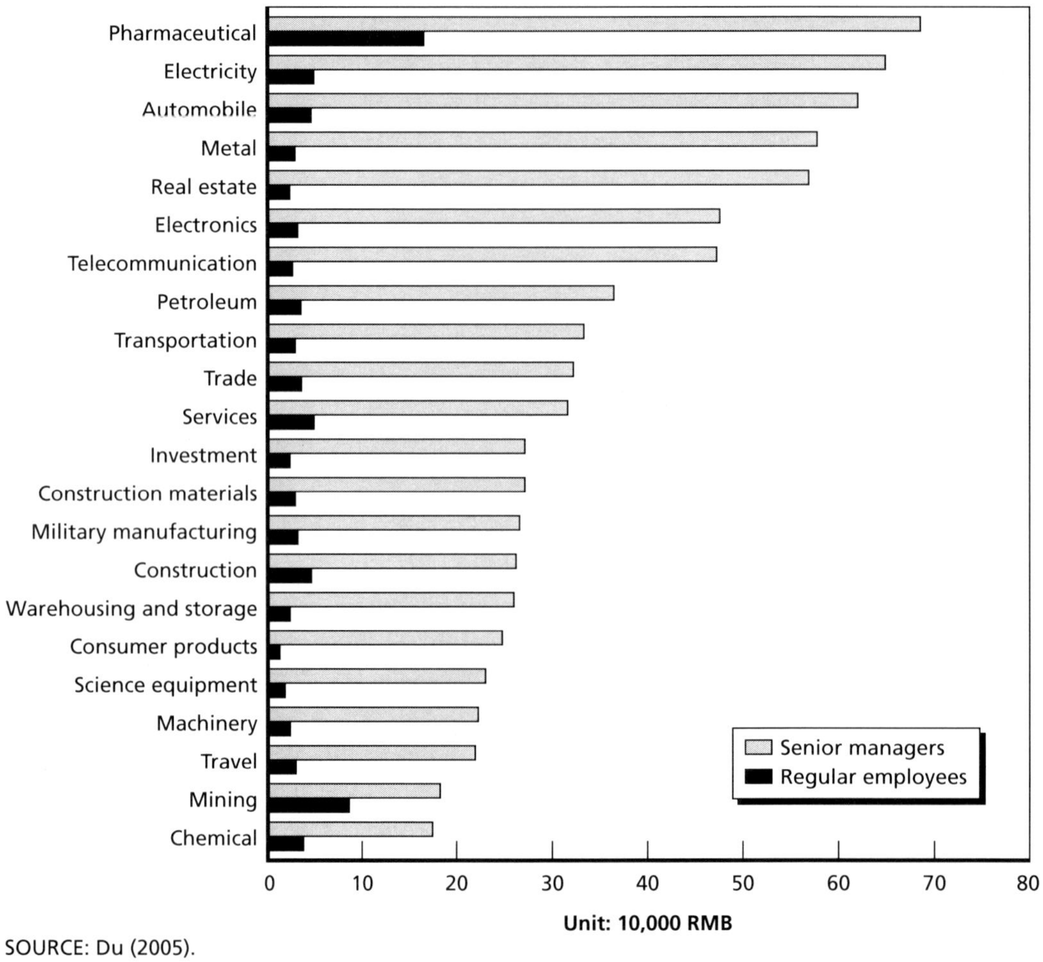

SOURCE: Du (2005).
RAND *TR618-3.3*

meals, but considering that many of these companies control the equivalent of billions of dollars in assets, it is hard to say that their executive nominal salaries are exceptionally high.

Nevertheless, some scholars argue that the current compensation system is not without flaw. Since a manager's compensation is heavily based on the company's performance in a single year, and his job security is uncertain, a manager might have a strong incentive to spur short-term returns without paying attention to the long-term growth of the company (Wang and Duan, 2006).

To better align the management's incentive with the company growth, the CSRC promulgated the Administrative Rules on Stock Incentives in Listed Companies (Trial) on December 31, 2005. Article 8 of these rules allows listed companies to issue stocks or stock options to senior management and important employees as incentives. Article 12 specifies that the accumulated amount of stocks and stock options issued cannot exceed 10 percent of the company's stock, and one awarded person cannot receive more than 1 percent of the total stock unless he or she has special permission from the general meeting of shareholders. According to a December 2006 survey, about 70 percent of listed companies were planning to use stock incentives in the next 12 months (*Shanghai Securities News*, 2006b).

Regulators

The central regulatory body for corporate governance of publicly listed companies is the CSRC. The CSRC, jointly with the State Council's Securities Commission (SCSC), was established by the State Council in October 1992 to regulate the newly created securities markets. SCSC enacted the macro policies, while the CSRC functioned as its executive agency and oversaw the market in accordance with the law. This arrangement persisted until 1998, when the State Council reformed and reorganized the securities regulatory framework and created the 1998 Securities Law. This move strengthened the CSRC by merging it with the SCSC and consolidating all other securities supervision activities under it. Over time, the CSRC's administrative and regulatory power was strengthened through various changes in its functions, internal structure, and personnel (CSRC, 2003).

The CSRC is a matrix organization with one chairman,[4] five vice chairmen, 16 functional departments, and three supporting centers. It also has 10 regional offices set up in key cities around the country, as well as a missionary office in every province and autonomous region in cities directly under the jurisdiction of the State Council and in cities enjoying provincial-level status in the state economic plan (CSRC, 2003). In total, the CSRC has about 1,800 staff members, whose average age is 35 years. About 40 percent of the staff have attained a masters degree or Ph.D. (CSRC, no date). The CSRC has been actively trying to attract people with an international background in securities regulation. For example, Laura Cha, a Hong Kong regulator, served for years as Deputy Chair of the CSRC. Gao Xiqing, a Chinese citizen who had become a dynamic New York lawyer, served in a similar capacity.[5]

In addition to fulfilling its regulatory duties, the goal of the CSRC is to promote transparency and good governance in the market and to create conditions that inspire investor confidence. It does this by regulating how shares are issued and traded on the stock exchanges, and by publishing regulations, circulars, standards, and guidelines that elaborate or clarify aspects of the Securities Law, the legal framework underlying the securities market. The CSRC regulates investment funds, fund managers, securities, and futures settlement companies and, in conjunction with the Bank of China, approves the qualification of fund custody institutions and formulates and implements rules on the qualification of senior management for the above-mentioned institutions. In addition, the CSRC carries out investigations to identify and prosecute securities fraud (Chen et al., 2005).

The CSRC has developed an international presence as the regulatory body representing China's markets overseas. It supervises the overseas investment activities of Chinese domestic firms, such as the overseas listing of shares or the establishment of securities institutions overseas. It also regulates the participation of foreign organizations in the domestic securities market, mostly through the Qualifying Foreign Institutional Investor (QFII) program.

---

4 As of October 2008, the chairman of the CSRC is Shang Fu-Lin, who has been in office since December 2002.

5 We thank William Overholt for making this comment.

The CSRC manages international cooperation and forms relationships through bilateral memoranda of understanding with regulatory bodies in other countries. For example, in May 2006, the U.S. Securities and Exchange Commission (SEC) and the CSRC jointly announced new "Terms of Reference for Enhanced Dialogue" (SEC, 2006b), which focuses on three objectives: (1) "corporate governance reforms, including requirements for audit committees, auditor independence and internal controls over financial reporting," (2) convergence of national accounting standards with international standards, and (3) the use of information technology to increase the value of financial reporting, including data tagging systems. Both regulatory agencies also planned to work toward increasing communication on cross-border regulatory issues, and the SEC planned to continue to provide training and technical assistance to the CSRC as its markets develop.

One of the CSRC's most important functions is to oversee the domestic stock exchanges. Whereas in many industrialized economies the stock exchanges are self-regulating organizations, the CSRC closely watches and vets the firms applying for listing. Before a firm can apply for listing on the stock exchange, a firm must first gain the approval of the CSRC. Thus the government agency plays a role as both a regulator and a developer of the Chinese stock markets. This role is unlike the "laissez faire" policy of the SEC in the U.S. exchanges, where the self-governing exchanges vet the firms and independently determine the market listing requirements. Once a firm passes the regulatory agency's screening, it must meet the general requirements of the stock exchanges, which are similar to those of international exchanges such as the New York Stock Exchange or the NASDAQ.

The CSRC has the power to take a range of different enforcement actions, depending on its assessment of the level and scope of a firm's or individual's infraction. It may issue a warning, confiscate stock, confiscate income gained illegally, issue a monetary penalty, or delist a firm found in violation of China's securities laws. According to Wind Data,[6] 60 stocks have been delisted from the markets since 1999. Like firms, individual violators may also be warned, lose their illegally gained incomes, receive a monetary penalty, or have their licenses or charters revoked. The stock exchanges also play a role in enforcement: for example, the SSE and SZSE stock exchanges may work with the firm or individual to correct the situation, rebuke a firm or individual publicly, or enforce the payment of a penalty. Punishments can also be issued to board directors, supervisors, listing sponsors, and secretaries of the boards of directors.

Many of the enforcement actions taken against Chinese firms are related to financial reporting. Chen et al. (2005) show that, among the infractions from 1999 to 2003, about 28 percent involved a major failure to disclose information, 18 percent involved a postponement or delay in disclosure, and another 18 percent involved false statements.

Unlike the SEC, the CSRC is responsible for both developing and regulating the capital market. The role of NGOs and self-regulation is very limited. According to Wang (2004), "All NGOs in China's securities market are de facto inferior subsidiaries of the CSRC. The two stock exchanges are no more than two departments of the CSRC, at least in the sense that their heads are appointed and their internal rules approved by the regulator."

Another difference between the CSRC and the SEC is that the SEC may bring a civil lawsuit against a company or an individual in cases where it uncovers securities fraud. The SEC's Division of Enforcement investigates possible violations of the federal securities laws, and pros-

[6] Wind Data is one of the largest providers of data on Chinese financial markets. See Wind Data (2007).

ecutes the commission's civil suits in federal court. In 2006, the SEC opened 914 investigations of the possible violations and brought 218 civil actions and 356 administrative proceedings against violating individuals and firms in the United States (SEC, 2006a). Although some have proposed that a similar system be adopted in China, there is little reason to believe it would be feasible under the current laws and judicial institutions. The CSRC is not allowed to sue violating companies or individuals in court. It achieves its regulatory goals mainly through administrative orders.

Auditing System

China's modern auditing system is relatively new, having evolved over the last 20 years. By comparison, the modern auditing system in Germany emerged in the late 1800s with the industrial revolution (Li, no date).

China's auditing system consists of activities in both the public and private sphere. The Ministry of Finance (MOF) formulates and implements accounting regulations and standards that apply to SOEs, listed firms, and private or family-owned businesses. The Chinese National Accounting Office (CNAO) carries out all internal government auditing activities and also performs auditing of the SOEs. Both the MOF and CNAO play a key and sometimes overlapping role in all auditing activities because of the complexity of the changing ownership status of the SOEs.

The MOF monitors the government's budget and accounting, oversees the activities of certified public accountants and accounting firms, and guides and regulates the auditing businesses, including those of foreign accounting firms. It serves both the public and private spheres of the auditing profession. The Department of Accounting Regulation at the MOF oversees most of these activities.

Even though the auditing system in China is primitive, the Chinese government has been eager to adopt international standards. For example, as mandated by a 2001 code issued by the CSRC, when companies issue initial public listings or reofferings, they must obtain "supplemental auditing" from an international accounting firm.[7] The MOF has also published numerous auditing and accounting standards in recent years in an attempt to further align China's standards with those accepted internationally. For example, the MOF released a new set of 48 auditing standards for certified public accountants, which aligns China's auditing rules more closely with the International Standards on Auditing (Centre for Financial Market Integrity, 2007). In addition, the MOF released new "Basic Accounting Standards for Business Enterprises" (ASBEs) in February 2006. The ASBEs consist of 38 standards that apply to all listed Chinese firms. The aim of this initiative is to facilitate further development of a market-like economy in China, raise the quality of financial information, and boost investor confidence. The ASBE standards are intended to bring Chinese accounting practices largely in line with the International Financial Reporting Standards. Although the new regulations have not achieved perfect convergence, they have achieved alignment in many areas and incorporated many key international principles. According to a report by Deloitte Touche Tohmatsu (2006), the revised ASBEs "cover nearly all of the topics under the current International Financial

---

[7] Guo and Ma (2004).

Reporting Standards (IFRS) literature" and thus significantly move China's standards toward "convergence" with international standards.

The Chinese Institute of Certified Public Accountants (CICPA) works closely with the MOF to oversee and regulate the certification of CPAs, and helps to ensure standards in the auditing profession. CICPA is a professional organization that establishes and maintains professional standards by administering the national CPA examinations, certifying CPAs, preparing professional guidelines and rules, and providing CPA education and training (CICPA, 2006). In addition to the regular requirements for CPAs, auditors must obtain special certification to audit securities-related business. This certification is administered by the Ministry of Finance and the CSRC through the National CPA Examination committee of the MOF.

CNAO, created in 1983, serves as the supreme audit institution of China and functions directly under the leadership of the prime minister. It organizes and administers the auditing work of the whole country; however, local audit institutions carry out auditing work in their respective provincial, municipal, and local jurisdictional levels in compliance with the 1994 Auditing Law and other related rules and regulations (National Audit Office of the People's Republic of China, no date–a). The CNAO is responsible for auditing the Central Government's budget implementation, as well as other governmental revenues and expenditures, and reports to the premier. The CNAO audits state and public institutions, including the Central Bank of China, state-owned monetary organizations, construction projects, SOEs, and "the enterprises and monetary organizations with State-owned capital controlling their shares or playing a leading role" as stipulated by the State Council (National Audit Office of the People's Republic of China, no date–b). Table 3.2 summarizes the auditing system in China.

Legal System

The role of the legal system in protecting investors' interests has been well documented in corporate governance literature (Shleifer and Vishny, 1997; La Porta et al., 1998, 1999, 2000). Legal scholars classify the world's legal systems into two groups based on their origins in the civil law system and the common law system. The former originates from ancient Roman law, which relies on statutes and comprehensive codes as the primary means of ordering legal material. In contrast, the latter resorts to precedents from judicial decisions, or cases, to gradually

Table 3.2
Auditing Requirements

Organization Type	Who Conducts the Audit?	Applicable Auditing Requirements/Laws
Listed firms	Approved CPA firms	MOF Order No. 33
Commercial banks	Approved CPA firms	MOF Order No. 33
Limited liability companies	Approved CPA firms	MOF Order No. 33
SOEs	CNAO	1994 Auditing Law
CSRC	CNAO	1994 Auditing Law
People's Bank of China	CNAO	1994 Auditing Law
Not-for-profit organizations	CNAO	1994 Auditing Law

shape the legal system. The legal system in China resembles the civil law group, but the judicial branch is not independent and is heavily influenced by administrative interventions.

The legal system in China is heavily understaffed. By 2002, there were only 180,000 judges and fewer than 120,000 lawyers in China, which translates to one judge for every 7,000 people and one lawyer for every 11,000 people. This is not only far less than in developed countries, but it is also less than in India, which in 2002 had about 500,000 lawyers, serving a population almost as large as that of China (Cabestan, 2002).

The Chinese legal system has been very weak in protecting investors. In the communist regime, private property was restricted. Private property rights were not legally recognized and protected in China until March 2007, when landmark legislation, the Property Law, was promulgated (effective after October 1, 2007). In addition, because of the lack of independence of the judicial branch, local judges are often appointed by district governments. Meanwhile, many listed companies are former SOEs, and central or local governments remain as controlling shareholders. Therefore, it is unrealistic to expect that the legal system will effectively protect the interest of individual investors without overcoming a lot of hurdles.

For example, the Supreme People's Court, the highest judicial branch in China, issued a decree in September 2001 stating that the courts would temporarily suspend civil compensation cases related to securities (Supreme People's Court of China, 2001). The decree acknowledged the existence of many securities frauds and insider trading, but decided not to allow courts to accept these cases. The Supreme People's Court cited two reasons for its decision: lack of legislative support and inexperienced human resources.[8] The Supreme People's Court amended the decree in January 2002 by accepting civil compensation claims as a result of false financial disclosure (Supreme People's Court of China, 2002). However, the court wouldn't take on any case until after the CSRC had investigated the claim and issued a penalty decision. Therefore, the court still did not have any real decision authority on securities cases and was treated as a weak enforcement entity.

Nevertheless, the court has started playing an increasingly important role in protecting shareholders. In January 2003, it published several provisions on the adjudication of civil suits for damages arising out of false representations in securities markets. Even though it still limited jurisdiction to cases related to false disclosure of company information, it removed the requirement for pre-judgment by the CSRC and allowed the court to take separate actions from the CSRC. Also, for the first time, it allowed a group of investors to form class actions to sue a company. The revised Company Law and Securities Law take another big step toward strengthening the role of the legal system in protecting investors. For example, Articles 20 and 21 of the Company Law stipulate that no shareholder, board director, or management executive can harm the interest of the company, other shareholders, or creditors. All losses shall be compensated by the violators according to law. The Securities Law also defines the legal responsibilities of market intermediaries and service companies, such as brokerage firms, financial auditors, investment advisors, and credit rating agents. If they disclose false information intentionally or fail to exert due diligence, they are subject to a fine of one to five times their received proceeds and may be banned from continuing business (Article 202 of the Securities Law). These legal provisions are expected to significantly expand the jurisdiction of the court beyond simply false disclosure. After five years of legal battles, the first case brought by

[8] "Zui Gao Fa Yuan: Zan Bu Shou Li Zheng Quan Min Shi Pei Chang An You Dao Li" (2001).

shareholders on false disclosure finally came to an end on December 4, 2006.[9] The sued listed company, Daqing Lianxi, paid 9.07 million RMB (about $1.1 million) to 381 shareholders (*Shanghai Securities News*, 2006a).

Stock Exchanges

An efficient stock market is important to economic growth (Levine, 1997; Levine and Zervos, 1998; Rajan and Zingales, 1998; Wurgler, 2000). In the era of the centrally planned economy, banks and other similar lending institutions (such as urban credit cooperatives, rural credit cooperatives, and credit unions) were virtually the sole source of financing in China. The two stock exchanges, SSE and SZSE, didn't open until the end of 1990.

SSE and SZSE have been long-time rivals to become China's financial center (Zhong, 2006; see Figure 3.4). After 1992, the Chinese government accelerated the development of Shanghai, and policies were tilted toward the city that once was the Gem of the Far East. Many multinational companies moved their area headquarters to Shanghai to tap into the huge Chinese domestic market. Shanghai is now starting to challenge Hong Kong as China's center for local financial products and is quickly becoming a preferred location of regional headquarters for many large multinational companies (Overholt, 2007). Meanwhile, SZSE has tried to model itself on the NASDAQ, focusing on high-tech and start-up companies. It opened the first Medium and Small Enterprises Trading Board in May 2004. Both SSE and SZSE have been growing rapidly, driven by the dramatic rally of the Chinese stock market since late 2005.

Figure 3.4
Market Capitalization of SSE and SZSE

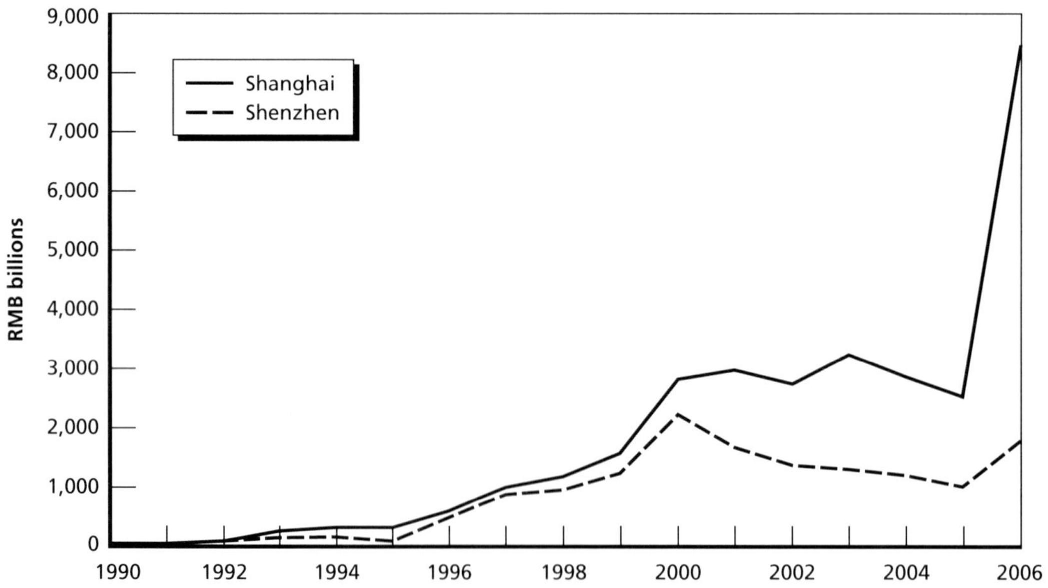

SOURCE: Wind Data (2007).
RAND *TR618-3.4*

[9] The final verdict of the lawsuit was made on December 28, 2004, but it took almost another two years to enforce the implementation.

According to the World Federation of Exchanges, SSE and SZSE ranked respectively the first and fourth fastest-growing exchanges in terms of market capitalization in 2006 (World Federation of Exchanges, 2006).

Both the Shanghai and Shenzhen stock exchange are nonprofit organizations governed by the CSRC. Their major responsibilities include

- providing markets for stock trading
- accepting applications to issue stock
- monitoring trading
- ensuring members' continuous compliance with relevant laws and regulations
- disclosing market and company information.

The stock exchanges are primarily a watchdog for the market; they don't have direct enforcement and punitive authority on non-complying companies (Institute of International Finance, 2006). The newly revised Securities Law added a few more administrative powers to the stock exchanges. Article 115 of the law entitles the exchanges to restrict trading of accounts in cases where they find significant irregular trading.

Both stock exchanges have to withdraw a certain proportion of all fees collected to form a risk fund (Article 116 of the Securities Law). The fund will be used to compensate investors from fraudulent stock trading. The specific withdrawal proportion and use of risk funds is monitored and regulated by the CSRC and the fiscal department of the State Council.

Chinese stock exchanges have an artificial limit imposed on the daily change of stock prices. In the early stages of the Chinese stock markets, investors often saw stock prices double or shrink by half in a single trading day. Because of rampant market manipulation and high price volatility, the Chinese government imposed a limit on stock prices in December 1996. Under this regulation, the maximum change, either upward or downward, of any stock is 10 percent of the closing price of the same stock in the previous trading day. If the price change of a stock reached this limit, its market transaction would be temporarily suspended until the next trading day. Studies on the impact of ceilings on price changes have been mixed. Supporters claim that Chinese capital markets are still primitive. Price limits can reduce market volatility and prevent some excessive speculative behaviors and thus protect small and medium investors (Liu et al., 2003). Others argue that this artificial limit reduces market efficiency and distorts the pricing mechanism. The system only temporarily suspends stocks' trading, which may translate into even bigger accumulative volatility in the long run (Chen and Long, 2003). As a solution, some researchers have suggested gradually increasing the daily limit on stock volatility (Chen, Fan, and Wong, 2003; Zuo and Gao, 2006).

Institutional Investors

Institutional investors play an important role in corporate governance. Individual investors usually don't have enough knowledge and experience to evaluate companies' management and it is often hard for them to act collectively and exert significant force on corporate governance issues. However, institutional investors typically have highly trained research and management teams that are better able to monitor and communicate with corporate management (Kim, Ho, and St Giles, 2003). In addition, what distinguishes institutional from retail investors is the size of their investment portfolios and their fiduciary responsibility to the institutions for which they make investments. As block holders of stocks, institutional investors can exert significant influence on corporate governance and management by sponsoring shareholder initiatives and by playing a role in the takeover voting processes in some firms. For example, in the 1980s, many U.S. institutional investors with endowments from universities and churches exerted economic and political pressure on South Africa by divesting from South African firms in order to protest the Apartheid system. Institutional investors have also helped to build capital markets by offering diversified investment options and by creating new financial products and services. Thus institutional investors are important for a healthy capital market.

The key institutional investors in China include mutual funds, insurance companies, social security funds, brokerage firms, and QFIIs (Figure 3.5). The size, share, and scope of China's institutional investors are still very small. For example, Kim, Ho, and St Giles (2003) estimate about 10 percent of the shares in China's equity markets are controlled by institutional owners, compared with about 60 percent in the United States (The Conference Board, 2007). According to OECD's estimate (accessed in May 2007), China's pension fund assets were 0.5 percent of GDP in 2005, whereas pensions fund assets in the United States were 98.9 percent of U.S. GDP. U.S. pension funds play a particularly important and stabilizing role in the U.S. market, accounting for about 40 percent of all U.S. institutional investor assets in 2005 (The Conference Board, 2007).

Social security funds only account for a small portion (around 4 percent) of institutional investment in China. This is in sharp contrast to developed countries. For example, Japan's insurance-and-pension sector attracts more than 25 percent of household savings. The small size of social security funds is due to the primitive stage of the market-based social security

Figure 3.5
Composition of Institutional Investors in China, by Market Capitalization

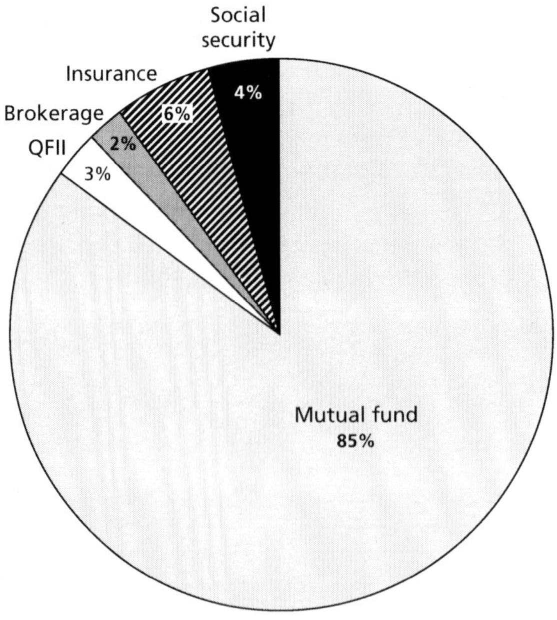

SOURCE: Wind Data (2007).
RAND *TR618-3.5*

system in China. Currently, social security funds have to be kept in state-owned commercial banks and managed under designated fiscal accounts. The balance of funds can only be used to buy treasury bonds or placed as deposits in banks, where interest earnings are negligible (Associated Press, 2006).

To invest in China, foreign institutional investors must be vetted and regulated by the CSRC under the QFII program. Qualified investors must have proven market management experience, must use only those financial instruments approved by the CSRC, must not exceed an ownership share of 10 percent of a single listed firm, and must keep their capital within the People's Republic of China for at least one year (Kim, Ho, and St Giles, 2003), among other regulations. However, even with many restrictions, QFIIs have been growing rapidly since the program's initiation. The CSRC's quota on QFII increased from $2.175 billion in 2003 to nearly $10 billion in 2007 (Figure 3.6). Even though QFII is still small compared relative to Chinese financial markets, Chinese investors have high expectations. They hope QFII can facilitate the improvement of the skills and standards of domestic institutional investors and play a more active role in monitoring companies' corporate governance (Kim, Ho, and St Giles, 2003).[10]

Another group of influential institutional shareholders is foreign strategic investors. Many Chinese commercial banks and large SOEs have actively engaged foreign strategic investors before they seek public listings in either domestic or international capital markets. Foreign investors are expected to bring new management skills to the system and to improve corpo-

Figure 3.6
CSRC Quota on Total Investment Amount Allowed by QFII Firms

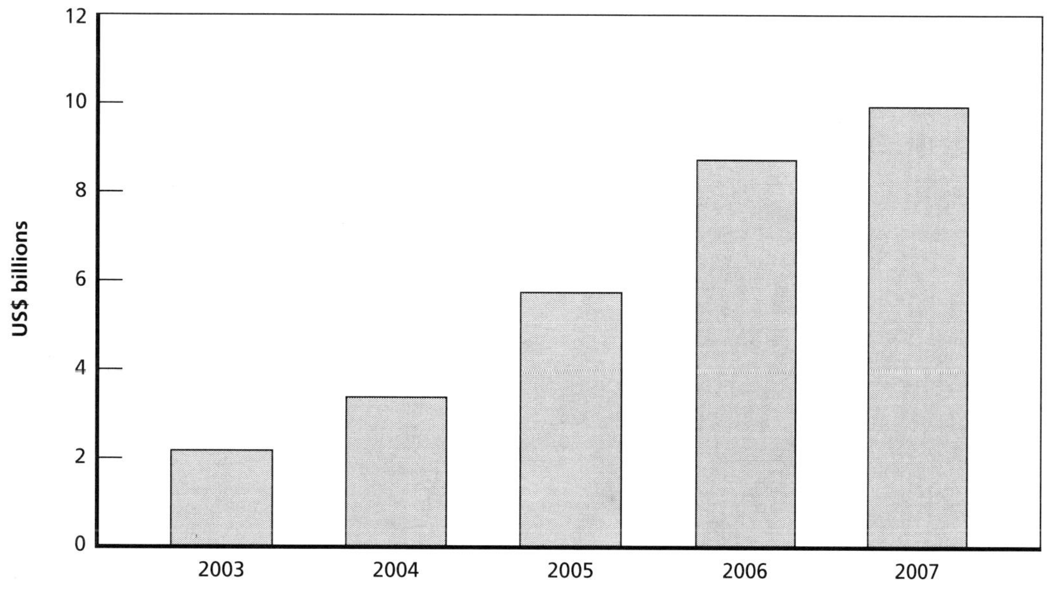

SOURCE: CSRC.

RAND *TR618-3.6*

[10] QFII and B-shares are related but they refer to different concepts. B-shares are denominated in RMB but can be bought and sold only in foreign currencies (such as U.S. dollars or Hong Kong dollars). Prior to 2001, B-shares were open only to foreigners and residents in Hong Kong, Taiwan, and Macao, but Chinese citizens have been allowed to trade B-shares since then. QFII is a special scheme that allows foreign financial institutions to participate in the Chinese stock markets, particularly the A-share market. Foreign financial institutions can buy and sell B-shares even if they *don't* have QFII permits, but they can trade A-shares only if they *are* in the QFII program.

rate governance (Okazaki, 2007). Since foreign strategic investors can usually obtain a certain number of seats on directors' boards, they can become a significant force in monitoring the company's management and exert a positive influence on corporate governance (Tang, 2005).

CHAPTER FOUR

Problems of Corporate Governance in China

Concentration of State Ownership

A 2007 annual report from Shanghai Stock Exchange shows that 65 percent of the listed companies are state enterprises (Liu, 2008), and in 2006, private companies were not permitted to list there (whereas 14 SOEs did). Although the total market capitalization of Chinese listed companies has reached 146–167 percent of China's GDP, more than two-thirds of this comes from state-owned, nontradable shares (Xie, 2007). Insiders of these SOEs are making large fortunes on the stock offerings. Although regulators have been fining or even delisting companies engaged in rent-seeking behavior, prosecutions for crimes such as insider trading are rare. A *Business Week* article cited a finance professor from Shanghai saying that "the central government wants a healthy stock market, but companies are owned by strong local and provincial governments, and they have more connections within the party" (Engardio et al., 2007, p. 38). Regulators either are afraid of going after local and provincial governments or may not have the power to go deeper. Foreign investment bankers still hold the view that the primary function of the Chinese stock market is to funnel money into state-owned companies. Information asymmetry and agency costs arise from the concentration of ownership of a company (Fama and Jensen, 1983). This practice has reduced the liquidity of the capital market and has discouraged minority investors from engaging in long-term investment.

An important negative impact from state ownership concentration is that the dominant state shareholder tends to divert resources from the jointly owned company. Liu and Sun (2005) also showed that partially listed companies tend to underperform wholly listed companies in China. It is our contention that wholly listed companies would be far less likely than their partially listed counterparts to engage in such value-destroying activities, because the former should have less propensity and fewer incentives to inefficiently transfer the capital they have raised from the equity market, since the whole company group has already been listed, whereas the partially listed companies may be very keen on diverting funds from their listed divisions to other subsidiaries.

In recent years, the protection of minority shareholders has been increasingly regarded as a priority for legislators of corporate governance (Liu, 2006; Sun and Tobin, 2005). Yet minority shareholders' interest, in general, has not been adequately protected. It is still widely believed among major state shareholders that minority shareholders do not have the right to disagree with the majority shareholder (Liu and Gao, 2000).

The downside of state-dominant ownership concentration also includes the weakness of institutional investors. Mutual funds made their debut in China's stock market as late as 1998 and have experienced a relatively slow growth during the years when China's listed companies grew by a double-digit rate. For example, social security funds can only invest a meager portion of their portfolio in the stock market, because pension funds have not yet been authorized by Chinese government to invest in the stock market and private equity has not yet been recognized as a legal entity in China. Consequently, 10 years after mutual funds appeared on the stage of the Chinese equity market, few of them have been able to join boards of directors in operating companies.

In November 2007, PetroChina surprised the world with its IPO in the Shanghai Stock Exchange by achieving the world's first market capitalization of more than a trillion dollars (Zhang, 2007). This achievement, however, was not without losses among minority investors in PetroChina's subsidiary companies. Prior to PetroChina's achievement, in November 2005 PetroChina announced an offer to buy back all the tradable shares of its three subsidiaries listed in Shanghai, with bidding prices only marginally higher than the quotes in 2005's bearish market (Zhou, 2005). This announcement was made after the share merger reform required all listed companies to fully circulate their nontradable shares. Given the context of share-merger reform ongoing in China, the buyback offer made by PetroChina Group was widely considered as predatory behavior to rob minority shareholders of their due claim to investment returns. Because the minority investors possessed less than 20 percent of these subsidiaries' equity, they could not prevent PetroChina from delisting its subsidiaries from the Shanghai Stock Exchange. For example, in 2005 there were 200 million tradable shares of Liaohe Oilfield, one of PetroChina's three listed subsidiaries. As these shares constituted only 18.18 percent of Liaohe Oilfield's total market capitalization, PetroChina only needed to win the agreement of 35 million tradable shares to complete the buyback and delisting deal. Three weeks after the announcement of PetroChina's buyback offer, the group received consent from less than 10 percent of the 35 million shares needed for the delisting. However, on November 22, 2005, suddenly more than 30 million shares agreed to the buyback offer, helping the conglomerate fulfill the condition to fully buy back Liaohe Oilfield with its announced price. A natural speculation of the weird pattern of equity buyback was that PetroChina struck some deals with institutional investors to achieve the buyback, but both PetroChina Group and its underwriter, China Galaxy Securities Co. Ltd., declined to comment. Two years after PetroChina bought back Liaohe Oilfield shares with a price-earning (P/E) ratio of 15.7, it opened its IPO day in November 2007 with a P/E ratio of 65 (Zhang, 2007). Given the 400 percent increase of the Shanghai Stock Exchange Index from 2005 to 2007, it is reasonable to view PetroChina's bidding price as a sign of its predatory buyback on November 22, 2005.

If PetroChina's buyback demonstrates the dominance of state ownership, the example of Baosteel's secondary offering and private placement in 2004 further illustrates the weakness of institutional investors in China (Wei, 2004). In August 2004, Baosteel Group, whose subsidiary Baosteel Co. Ltd. was a major state-owned company listed in the Shanghai Stock Exchange, announced a plan to transform the entire group into a listed company. The plan included a secondary offering in the Shanghai Stock Exchange and a private placement that would increase Baosteel Group's holdings in Baosteel Co. Ltd. The announcement specified that the shares sold to the public through a secondary offering would not exceed those sold to Baosteel Group through a private placement, but did not specify the exact ratio of tradable shares to nontradable shares. Nor did Baosteel Co. Ltd. specify its plan for a secondary equity offering for the current shareholders. The risk implied by this ambiguous announcement incurred widespread anger among Baosteel Co. Ltd.'s minority shareholders, and two major Chinese financial media conglomerates led petitions against Baosteel's plan. Given the proportion of those investors in Baosteel's tradable shares in 2004, the shareholders did have veto power on the announced Baosteel plan. The institutional investors in Baosteel generally expressed a preference for more favorable conditions from Baosteel Co. Ltd., so Chinese financial analysts expected that the shareholders' general meeting in September would witness a veto. On the contrary, after a few private meetings between Baosteel managers and fund managers prior to the shareholder general meeting, no institutional investors voted against the plan at the September meeting. Consequently, the plan was passed and later the minority shareholders incurred considerable losses. The press later exposed that Baosteel had promised commissions to the fund managers, which could have served as leverage to avoid a unanimous veto from the institutional investors. This example demonstrates that even the involvement of institutional investors does not guarantee protection of the short-run interests of minority shareholders in China's current legal environment.

As suggested above, one important factor that has seriously hindered the impact of institutional investors on monitoring corporate governance is the large chunk of nontradable shares controlled by the state. The share merger reform implemented in 2005 was intended to address this issue. According to McKinsey's estimate, all shares in China's SOEs will become fully tradable by 2012 (Ahn and Cogman, 2007). Institutional investors will be more likely to replace the state or local governments as the majority shareholders in many large enterprises. This should exert a positive influence on corporate governance.

Weak Supervisory Board and Independent Directors

A direct result of ownership concentration is the lack of independence among board directors. According to the 1993 Company Law, the shareholders' general meeting holds the right to elect or remove board directors; however, the law doesn't specify the nomination process. In the absence of legal specification, it is easy for the dominant owner, often the Chinese government, to nominate all the directors for a company. With strong government involvement, the chosen directors could be symbolic figures chosen to meet the legal requirement for a listed company. In a 1999 survey of listed companies, Tenev and Zhang (2002) found that only 3.1 percent of all directors had some degree of independence; the vast majority of directors remain under the dominant influence of the government. Without director independence, the call for fiduciary duty and duty of care will be ineffective. Thus before directors can effectively carry out their duties, a fundamental change in the power structure of company boards needs to take place.

Given the overwhelming dominance of the government's influence on boards of directors, the supervisory board in China has not yet played a significant and effective governance role (Tam, 2002; Tenev and Zhang, 2002). Since bureaucrats in charge of the company nominate and remove directors and supervisors alike, members of the supervisory board have little say in the major corporate decisions, particularly when their role of overseeing the board of directors has been only vaguely defined in China's Company Law. No law gives supervisors the right to take civil litigation against board directors or senior managers when they detect company misconduct. Moreover, the supervisors are usually selected from the company's employees or are former communist cadres in the state-owned enterprise who could not fit in other positions in a corporatized organization, and therefore their financial interests are directly determined by the very people they are supposed to supervise (Zheng, 2003). Statistics show that on average, members of the board of supervisors are significantly less educated than members of the board of directors, and most of the supervisors are not experienced enough in accounting and management to perform checks and balances vis-à-vis the board of directors and senior managers.

As we discussed in Chapter Two, in August 2001 the CSRC required that independent directors constitute at least one-third of the board of directors in each listed company, probably as a common law solution to the prevalent powerlessness of supervisory boards. Every listed company had to meet the requirement by June 2003. The supposedly impartial role of independent directors might serve as a complement to the supervisory board in a Chinese listed company; however, this common law solution has been difficult to implement because China does not have enough qualified people to fill the role of independent directors. The new rule called for around 5,000 independent directors to join China's listed companies in less than two years. Notably, the skills required for effective independent directors cannot easily be developed by vocational training, nor can Chinese companies easily find Chinese-speaking talents from overseas to assume the sensitive position of independent director. Instead, independent directors must either be grown from within, which requires time, or be imported from outside China, which can be very costly. And, as we observed in Chapter Two, inexperienced independent directors have been fairly weak (since 1998) in their ability to influence or control corporate management, despite their legally endowed power to do so.

Insider Trading

Article 67 of China's Securities Law prohibits persons with knowledge of insider information from using such information to trade securities. Article 68 lists those who are considered "persons with knowledge of inside information." They include

1. directors, supervisors, managers, deputy managers, and other senior management persons concerned with companies that issue shares or corporate bonds
2. shareholders who hold not less than 5 percent of the shares in a company
3. the senior management persons of the holding company of a company that issues shares
4. persons who are able to obtain material company information concerning the trading of its securities by virtue of the positions they hold in the company
5. staff members of the securities regulatory authority, and other persons who administer securities trading pursuant to their statutory duties
6. the relevant staff members of public intermediary organizations who participate in securities trading pursuant to their statutory duties and the relevant staff members of securities registration and clearing institutions and securities trading service organizations
7. other persons specified by the securities regulatory authority under the State Council.

The same Securities Law, however, does not say anything about specific private liability for people involved with insider trading, which has become a very serious problem among China's listed companies (Wu and Tang, 2003). An (2004) noted that the punishment of insider trading cases in China tends to be minuscule compared with the profit gained from such deals, citing a case in which a Chinese investment banker was fined only 50,000 yuan after the CSRC found out about his million-dollar insider deal.

Tomasic and Andrews (2006) attributed the rampant insider trading in China to two factors: the lack of concept for fiduciary duty and inefficient enforcement. China has not reached a commonly agreed translation of the legal concept "fiduciary duty." Although Article 62 in *Regulatory Views on Limited-Liability Shareholding Companies* (1992) ruled that board members do bear fiduciary duty (*chengxin yiwu*, as interpreted by Liu and Gao, 2000), the imported notion of common law liability did not fit in well with China's civil law tradition. With neither common law precedents nor civil law definitions in place, many Chinese shareholders and managers are not fully aware of the necessity of avoiding conflicts of interest in corporate context. Similarly, it is difficult for judges to tell whether a person has failed to observe fiduciary duty without applicable Chinese precedents and civil law specifications.

In regard to inefficient enforcement, Tomasic and Andrews (2006) also noted that the Australian Securities and Investments Commission (ASIC) employed 1,396 full-time-equivalent staff to serve a population of 2 million citizens in 2001, while in the same year there were only about 1,465 CSRC staff working to serve a population of 68 million investors. A different personnel problem in enforcement can be found among Chinese judges, who generally lack adequate knowledge and experience to deal with everyday company cases (due to the young age of Chinese stock market), let alone far more nuanced cases, such as those involving insider trading.

Another reason why insider trading remains uncurbed could be the absence of class actions in China. Unlike in the United States, where private enforcement of insider trading regulations considerably compensates aggrieved issuers and shareholders for the inadequacy of government enforcement, class actions are still strongly discouraged in China (Supreme People's Court of China, 2002). Although in recent years class actions have been used in various kinds of civil litigation in China, and lawyer-initiated cases have been filed against such listed Chinese companies and accounting giants as Deloitte Touche Tohmatsu (Lu, 2006), we have not been able to find an application on the front of investor protection. Also, unlike the United States, China has created no incentive mechanism to encourage reporting or whistle-blowing about insider trading, which might offset part of the risk involved (Li, 2007).

Fabrication of Financial Reports Among Listed Companies

Since January 2001, the Supreme People's Court of China (SPC) has made considerable progress in setting up a framework for private securities litigation to allow investors to sue listed companies for losses caused by their false financial disclosures (Tomasic and Andrews, 2006). The SPC has developed procedural and substantive rules for the filing and adjudication of such suits, and over 1,000 suits have been filed nationwide against some 14 companies. Although a number of these actions have been settled out of court, most remain in legal limbo, with courts refusing to make judgment, and none have been settled by a court judgment in favor of the investors. First, the framework creates some serious obstacles for investors wanting to pursue actions. The physical location of where the suit can be filed, the narrowly defined causal link between false statements made by the company and losses experienced by investors, and the preliminary requirement that the CSRC or other relevant government bodies find against the firm (or issue a criminal verdict against the board directors) do not help. Moreover, the lack of a class action (*jituan susong*) framework, and the mechanics of a group suit (*gongtong susong*) create considerable legal difficulties for would-be plaintiffs, as hundreds of investors have to coordinate their actions across considerable distance. Secondly, local courts usually appeared unwilling to have these cases become known to the press because of administrative protection of firms by local governments. The few actions that did lead to favorable results to the investors were cases settled out of court. However, it is unlikely that many of these cases will result in compensation to investors under the current scheme, and the most important aspect of developments so far has been the creation of a potential personal liability for directors, which may discourage them from making false disclosures in the future.

Outside of the courts, aspects of the accounting profession and news media in China likely also contribute to a climate in which false financial reporting can proliferate. For example, Xiao, Zhang, and Xie (2000) illuminated some major features of the Chinese audit market, such as the lack of audit independence, the shortage of well-qualified auditors, and an environment of massive corruption. As Doe and Chan (2001) noted from a Ministry of Finance report in China, a significant number of Chinese companies forged their earnings in annual reports for the preceding accounting year in 2001. Although this could be a one-sided story that differs from what the CSRC would say, the observation made by the Ministry of Finance, a government body in charge of accounting and taxation, nevertheless reflects the seriousness of corporate fabrication of financial information. Certified public accounting emerged as a profession in China only after the birth of China's stock markets. The severe undersupply of CPAs in the 1990s resulted in the certification of a large number of inexperienced public accounts. Today, the majority of China's CPAs lack sufficient knowledge about international accounting practices (Lin, 2004) and are not experienced enough to cope adequately with corporate fraud. So far, there has been no specific legislation delineating the punishment for CPAs who are involved in accounting fraud with listed companies.

Finance, sports, entertainment, and technology have been key areas where the Chinese press has made significant but gradual progress in their freedom of reporting and commenting (Shi, 2003). Chinese newspapers and magazines have also played an active role in exposing corporate fraud and pushing corporate governance legislation. At the same time, progress made in the financial news cannot greatly outpace the gradual progress in other news categories. A significant number of corporate frauds find their roots in senior officials who exert significant influence on the hiring decisions of journalists or even the licensing of the medium itself. Therefore, a considerable proportion of discussions about corporate governance eventually end up in Internet chatrooms and cell phone messages. This phenomenon adds to the speculative nature of China's capital market and hurts the investor's confidence in China's corporate world in general.

Immature Capital Market

China's immature capital market is characterized by the Chinese banks' preferential treatment of state-owned enterprises, the difficulty in issuing corporate bonds, and the lack of preferred shares. For capital input, listed companies in China overwhelmingly rely on preferential loans from banks and issuing common shares with high P/E ratios, with neither of these two sources of capital effectively responding to the quality of corporate performance. By the end of the third quarter of 2007, "enterprise bonds" (*qiyezhai*) took up only 3.22 percent of China's debt market, significantly less than the treasury bonds and financial bonds. The issuance of these enterprise bonds has been subject to governmental approval on a case-by-case basis, and has been used to serve such purposes as infrastructure building and industrial policies (Li, 2007). Similarly, although there was discussion about issuing preferred shares in the early 1990s, this investment option has never formally appeared in China's security market. Nor has shorting been formally possible in the Shanghai and Shenzhen stock exchanges. The consequence is that buying common shares has remained as the one and only "option" for securities investors in China, and investors have few safer choices to make as they look for alternatives to bank deposits.

In 1999 it seemed that the Shenzhen Stock Exchange would take up the role of the NASDAQ in China, and the Shanghai Stock Exchange would perform as the Chinese counterpart of the NYSE, because the central government granted the Shenzhen Stock Exchange the opportunity to serve technology start-ups, while other IPOs were limited to Shanghai. Although the latter policy was adopted and the Shenzhen Stock Exchange stopped listing new companies after 1999, the former policy was surprisingly tabled by the then Premier Zhu Rongji, who expressed a concern for the risk involved with high-tech start-ups. Consequently, the market capitalization in the Shenzhen Stock Exchange gradually shrank to less than one-fourth of that in the Shanghai Stock Exchange, and the latter began to assume a monopoly role in China's equity market.

On a related note, when China banned underground over-the-counter trading in 1999, companies generally had only one choice when making public offerings in mainland China. The government-imposed quota on annual IPOs led to a severe undersupply of IPO opportunities. A dramatic example was that a listed company often found its share price skyrocketing when it reported continuous financial losses and could face a removal from the stock exchange because continuous financial loss meant a high probability of buyout, regardless of the company's real value. In other words, the listing of a company in mainland China's stock exchange is a very scarce resource and could lead to rampant rent-seeking behavior for the government and the listed company, as well as an abundant opportunity for insider trading and speculation. Thus, it is not difficult to understand why there has been a notoriously high average P/E ratio in China's stock market and why share prices in China might not mean much for the performance of listed companies. The absence of over-the-counter trading and bond trading, coupled with a strict quota for company listing, has both limited capital supply for the Chinese companies not listed in the stock market and twisted the performance evaluation for the Chinese companies that are. In recent years, the difficulty of obtaining permission for an IPO in the Chinese stock market has led high-tech Chinese enterprises to the NASDAQ, although they incur additional costs associated with the cross-cultural information asymmetry.

CHAPTER FIVE

Conclusion

Despite the rapid progress China has been making in corporate governance, serious problems abound in various aspects of Chinese institutions and practices, ranging from ownership structure in Chinese companies to the national news media environment. The main obstacles come from the following four areas:

1. A shortage of experienced personnel to serve as government officials, company managers, members of supervisory boards, independent directors, certified public accountants, and lawyers specialized in corporate laws. This problem results from the short history of the Chinese market economy, and it may improve as professionals grow and learn from their experiences and Chinese companies accelerate their globalization processes.
2. The overwhelming dominance of state ownership in shareholding companies. This problem evolved from the once-controlled economy, and it may improve as the ongoing share merger reform continues to release state shares to the market and institutional investors gradually gain strength.
3. The immaturity of the market economy, including the absence of an over-the-counter (OTC) securities market and corporate debt market.
4. The institutional confinement of check-and-balance mechanisms in China, including the absence of class actions and the weak watchdog role of mass media. This problem may remain unchanged for the foreseeable future.

In consequence, we present a cautiously optimistic scenario for tomorrow's corporate governance in China, because the gradual removal of ownership and personnel barriers, coupled with an increasingly globalized and mature business environment, will eventually improve governance, even though the existent institutional limitations might slow the progress. Part of our optimism is also based on the globalization of Chinese listed companies, such as those being listed in Hong Kong, which has pushed them toward international standards of corporate governance (Sun and Tobin, 2005; Mar and Young, 2001). Starting in the 1990s, a number of major Chinese companies with sound profit records started IPOs in overseas markets, including Hong Kong and New York. This trend grew to a larger scale as China's high-tech and financial sector emerged in overseas capital markets. Sun and Tobin (2005) remark that SOEs such as the Bank of China increased their transparency and accountability after their public listings in Hong Kong and improved their performance. For those companies listed overseas, the "Hong Kong effects" on their corporate governance translated into better transparency and accountability back home in the mainland stock market. Since the Chinese government has intentionally pushed China's best companies to raise investment from overseas stock markets, these companies are often simultaneously listed in the mainland stock market to attract investors with their "world-class performance." Therefore, globalization can be seen as a positive force that has accelerated corporate governance reform in China. Furthermore, in August 2007, the government announced a decision to allow mainland Chinese citizens to invest in non-mainland stock markets, particularly in Hong Kong. Although details of implementation still have not been disclosed as of October 2008, this policy offers the potential to improve Chinese corporate governance, because mainland enterprises will need to compete with their Hong Kong counterparts for investors.

Beyond the general trend toward increasing global influence and gradually improving corporate governance institutions and practices, a number of more specific policy proposals have been offered to further strengthen governance mechanisms in China. For example, Lin (2004) proposed several policy levers that could be implemented within China's current institutional framework, for example, clearly defining the functions of the Supervisory Board, making it easier for individual investors to sue management, and toughening legal obligations for managers involved in insider trading. Tenev and Zhang (2002) proposed lowering the minimum required number of shares for shareholders to raise proposals, and increasing the legal obligations of controlling shareholders. Another proposed policy is to develop a long-term focus incentive/compensation system for directors and executives, such as long-term nontradable options (Lin, 2001).

We would also propose the revival and institutionalization of the once-banned regional OTC markets, because it would offer an opportunity to improve the corporate governance of Chinese enterprises and provide a buffer zone for those facing the risk of delisting in Shanghai and Shenzhen Stock Exchanges. The function of buffer-zoning is to make delisting an easier decision for the stock exchanges, and a more acceptable scenario for the delisted company. It also decreases the risk for the investors in high-risk enterprises. Similarly, accelerating the development of a corporate debt market in China could also help meet the needs of the more risk-averse investors, and thus increase the capital supply for Chinese companies in need of steady capital input.[1]

We also suggest establishing an incentive mechanism to encourage reporting of insider trading. Future efforts to improve the organizational performance of the CSRC and the Chinese stock exchanges will require considerable time and resources, as well as promulgation of the concept of fiduciary duty. In contrast, we anticipate that providing incentives for exposing insider trading may cost less and could be more effective in China than in the United States because of Chinese professionals' relatively low incomes.

In summary, corporate governance in China has improved significantly since the economic reforms began, but many problems remain. Continuing to improve corporate governance is vital for China's economic growth. We believe that this is also an important area for future research. Some potential questions for future study include

---

[1] After several years' pondering by the central government, Tianjin Binhai New Area (TBNA) finally received an approval in late March 2008 to establish the first OTC market in China (Xinhua, 2008). Even though a detailed schedule has yet to be seen, the Tianjin OTC market is expected to serve as the third major financial center in China, as a complement to the two stock exchanges in Shanghai and Shenzhen. If the OTC market is successfully launched, companies in China will have more flexible and diverse ways to participate in the capital markets.

- What is the empirical evidence concerning the relationship between corporate governance and financial performance in China? Are better-governed companies recognized and rewarded by the financial markets? Has the relationship changed over time, as corporate governance has received more and more attention in China?
- What are the impacts of foreign strategic investors on Chinese corporate governance? To what extent can foreign investors influence corporate governance of Chinese companies?
- When Chinese companies are listed on foreign stock markets, can investors trust that these companies have appropriate corporate governance mechanisms in place and that investor interests are dutifully guarded? If the Chinese government still owns substantial shares of overseas listed companies, should foreign investors take additional precautions when making investment decisions?
- Does the recent dramatic drop of China's stock markets have any relation to corporate governance issues? How so?
- What are the roles that the government should play in improving corporate governance? Besides pushing out new codes and regulations, can the government take more market-based approaches, such as educating individual investors and enhancing the monitoring role of the media?
- How does corporate governance in China compare with that in other developing countries, for example, India and Thailand? Some researchers have already started to study corporate governance in an international, comparative context (for example, see Rajagopalan and Zhang, 2008), and we believe many insights can be gained through such comparisons.

References

Ahn, J., and D. Cogman, "A Quiet Revolution in China's Capital Markets," *McKinsey on Finance*, Vol. 24, 2007, pp. 18–24.

An, M., "A Low-Cost, Low-Risk Seduction? Insider Trading as Viewed from the CNAF Case," *Guoji Jinrong Bao* [International Finance News], December 20, 2004.

Associated Press, "China Audit Finds $900M in Misused Funds," *International Business Times*, November 24, 2006.

Bai, C. E., Q. Liu, J. Lu, F. M. Song, and J. Zhang, "Corporate Governance and Market Valuation in China," *Journal of Comparative Economics*, Vol. 32, No. 4, 2004, pp. 599–616.

Berle, A., and G. C. Means, *The Modern Corporation and Private Property*, New York, Macmillan Publishing Co., 1932.

Cabestan, Jean-Pierre, BBC News (in Chinese), July 24, 2002. As of October 7, 2008:
http://news.bbc.co.uk/chinese/simp/hi/newsid_2140000/newsid_2149200/2149206.stm

Cadbury Report—*See* Committee on the Financial Aspects of Corporate Governance.

Centre for Financial Market Integrity, *China Corporate Governance Survey*, 2007. As of October 6, 2008:
http://www.cfapubs.org/toc/ccb/2007/2007/3

Charreaux, G., and P. Desbrieres, "Corporate Governance: Stakeholder Value Versus Shareholder Value," *Journal of Management and Governance*, Vol. 5, No. 2, 2001, pp. 107–128.

Chen, D. H., J. P. H. Fan, and T. J. Wong, "Do Politicians Jeopardize Professionalism? Decentralization and the Structure of Chinese Corporate Boards," Hong Kong, China: Hong Kong University of Science and Technology, working paper, 2003.

Chen, G., M. Firth, D. N. Gao, O. M. Rui, "Is China's Securities Regulatory Agency a Toothless Tiger? Evidence from Enforcement Actions," *Journal of Accounting and Public Policy*, Vol. 24, No. 6, 2005, 451–488.

Chen, J., "Ownership Structure as Corporate Governance Mechanism: Evidence from Chinese Listed Companies," *Economics of Planning*, Vol. 34, 2001, pp. 53–72.

Chen, P., and H. Long, "Price Limits Performance in Stock Market of China: Evidence and Suggestions," *World Economy* (in Chinese), Vol. 2, 2003, pp. 56–65.

China Securities Regulatory Commission, "About the CSRC" (in Chinese), no date. As of October 22, 2008:
http://www.csrc.gov.cn/n575458/n575667/n641473/index.html

———, "Introduction of CSRC," Web page, 2003. As of October 7, 2008:
http://211.154.210.238/en/homepage/about_en.jsp

Committee on the Financial Aspects of Corporate Governance, *Financial Aspects of Corporate Governance* [The Cadbury Report], London, 1992. As of October 6, 2008:
http://www.ecgi.org/codes/documents/cadbury.pdf

The Conference Board, "U.S. Institutional Investors Continue to Boost Ownership of U.S. Corporations," press release, January 22, 2007. As of October 7, 2008:
http://www.conference-board.org/UTILITIES/pressDetail.cfm?press_ID=3046

Deloitte Touche Tohmatsu, "China's New Accounting Standards: A Comparison with Current PRC GAAP and IFRS," 2006.

Di, W., X. L. Ren, and Z. H. Wang, "Comments on Strengthening Corporate Governance," *Business Economics* (in Chinese), Vol. 6, 2005, pp. 45–46.

Doe, J., and W. W. Y. Chan, "Towards Better Corporate Governance: China's Continuing Struggle," *International Financial Law Review*, London, 2001, pp. 21–28.

Du, L., "Revelation of Managers of Enterprises Owned by Central Government," *China Entrepreneur*, Vol. 8, 2005, pp. 26 29.

Ellman, M., "China's OTC Markets," *Comparative Economic Studies*, Vol. 30, 1988, pp. 59–64.

Engardio, P., D. Roberts, F. Balfour, and B. Einhorn, "Broken China," *Business Week*, Vol. 4043, July 23, 2007.

Fama, E. F., and Jensen, M. C., "Separation of Ownership and Control," *Journal of Law and Economics*, Vol. 26, 1983, pp. 301–325.

Green, S., "Enterprise Reform and Stock Market Development in Mainland China," *Deutsche Bank Research*, March 25, 2004.

Groves, T., Y. Hong, J. McMillan, and B. Naughton, "Autonomy and Incentives in China State Enterprises," *Quarterly Journal of Economics,* Vol. 109, February 1994, pp. 183–209.

Guo, Hong Chao, and Yi Ma, "Shou Fei de Tian Shang Di Xia [The Huge Difference in Charges]," *Economic Observer*, November 25, 2004. As of October 22, 2008:
http://sjj.sh.gov.cn/node2/node9/node31/u1a6736.html

Ho, S. S. M., "Corporate Governance in China," Hong Kong Baptist University, working paper, 2003.

Hua, J., P. Miesing, and M. Li, "An Empirical Taxonomy of SOE Governance in Transitional China," *Journal of Management and Governance*, Vol. 10, No. 4, 2006, pp. 401–433.

Huang, Y., W. T. Woo, K. P. Kalirajan, and R. Duncan, "Enterprise Reform, Technological Progress and Technical Efficiency in China's State Industry," National Centre for Development Studies, Australian National University, Canberra, 1998.

Institute of International Finance, *Corporate Governance in China: An Investor Perspective*, Washington, D.C., 2006.

Jensen, M. C., and W. H. Meckling, "Theory of the Firm: Managerial Behavior, Agency Costs and Ownership Structure," *Journal of Financial Economics*, Vol. 3, No. 4, 1976, pp. 305–360.

Johnson, S., P. Boone, A. Breach, and E. Friedman, "Corporate Governance in the Asian Financial Crisis," *Journal of Financial Economics*, Vol. 58, Nos. 1–2, 2000, pp. 141–186.

Kim, Y., I. S. M. Ho, and M. St Giles, "Developing Institutional Investors in People's Republic of China," Washington, D.C.: World Bank, World Bank Country Study Paper, 2003.

"Lao Ba Gu: Cheng Tou Bian Huan Da Wang Qi" [The Come-and-Go of Tycoons], *Competitiveness*, March 11, 2005. As of October 22, 2008:
http://finance.sina.com.cn/stock/t/20050311/12071422984.shtml

La Porta, R., F. Lopez-de-Silanes, and A. Shleifer, "Corporate Ownership Around the World," *Journal of Finance,* Vol. 54, No. 2, 1999, pp. 471–517.

La Porta, R., F. Lopez-de-Silanes, A. Shleifer, and R. Vishny, "Law and Finance," *Journal of Political Economy*, Vol. 106, No. 6, 1998, pp. 1113–1155.

———, "Investor Protection and Corporate Governance," *Journal of Financial Economics*, Vol. 58, No. 1, 2000, pp. 3–27.

Levine, R., "Financial Development and Economic Growth: Views and Agenda," *Journal of Economic Literature*, Vol. 35, No. 2, 1997, pp. 688–726.

Levine, R., and S. Zervos, "Stock Markets, Banks, and Economic Growth," *American Economic Review*, Vol. 88, No. 3, 1998, pp. 537–558.

Li, L., "Corporate Bonds Entered the Capital Market," *Fortune Life,* December 24, 2007.

Li, W., "The Impact of Economic Reform on the Performance of Chinese State Enterprises, 1980–1989," *Journal of Political Economy*, Vol. 105, No. 5, 1997, pp. 1080–1106.

Li, X., "Americans Reporting Insider Trading Can Claim 10% of the Illegal Profit," *Caijing Magazine*, April 2007.

Li, Y., "A Comparative Study About Internal Auditing Approach Between Germany and China," Chengdu City, China: Southwestern University of Finance and Economics, no date. As of October 7, 2008: http://aaahq.org/audit/midyear/06midyear/papers/Li.doc

Lin, C., "Corporatisation and Corporate Governance in China's Economic Transition," *Economics of Planning*, Vol. 24, Nos. 1–2, 2001, pp. 5–35.

Lin, T. W., "Corporate Governance in China: Recent Developments, Key Problems, and Solutions," *Journal of Accounting and Corporate Governance*, Vol. 1, June 2004, pp. 1–23.

Liu, G. S., and P. Sun, "The Class of Shareholdings and Its Impacts on Corporate Performance: A Case of State Shareholding Composition in Chinese Public Corporations," *Corporate Governance: An International Review*, Vol. 13, No. 1, 2005, pp. 46–59.

Liu, H. R., and X. Q. Gao, "For the Establishment of H Shares," *China-Review.com* (in Chinese), October 16, 2000. As of October 6, 2008:
http://www.china-review.com/gao.asp?id=10899

Liu, Q., "Corporate Governance in China: Current Practices, Economic Effects and Institutional Determinants," *CESifo Economic Studies*, Vol. 52, No. 2, 2006, pp. 415–453.

Liu, S., "An Analysis of the Actual Company Controllers from the 2007 Annual Reports," *Shanghai Security Times*, June 6, 2008.

Liu, Y. H., J. H. He, et al., "Evidence for China Stock Market: Changing Volatility Under a Price Limit Regime," *Management Sciences* (in Chinese), Vol. 16, No. 5, 2003, pp. 48–53.

Lu, Z. M., "Practical Implications of Collective Action Against Deloitte Touche Tohmatsu," *Beijing News*, April 11, 2006.

Mar, P., and M. N. Young, "Corporate Governance in Transition Economies: A Case Study of Two Chinese Airlines," *Journal of World Business*, Vol. 36, No. 3, 2001, pp. 280–302.

Megginson, W. L., and J. M. Netter, "From State to Market: A Survey of Empirical Studies on Privatization," *Journal of Economic Literature*, Vol. 39, No. 2, 2001, pp. 321–389.

National Audit Office of the People's Republic of China, "Brief History of Audit in China," Web page, no date–a. As of October 7, 2008:
http://www.cnao.gov.cn/main/articleshow_ArtID_725.htm

———, "Duties and Responsibilities of Audit Institutions in China," Web page, no date–b. As of October 7, 2008.
http://www.cnao.gov.cn/main/articleshow_ArtID_728.htm

National Bureau of Statistics of the People's Republic of China, *China Statistical Yearbook 2008*, 2008.

Naughton, B., "Chinese Institutional Innovation and Privatization from Below," *American Economic Review Papers and Proceedings*, Vol. 84. No. 2, 1994, pp. 266–270.

Ning, X. D., "Threshold for Shareholders Involvement," *IT Management World* (in Chinese), September 2006, p. 96.

Okazaki, K., *Banking System Reform in China: The Challenges of Moving Toward a Market-Oriented Economy*, Santa Monica, Calif.: RAND Corporation, OP-194-CAPP, 2007.

Organisation for Economic Co-operation and Development, *OECD Principles of Corporate Governance*, Paris: OECD Publishing, 2004.

Overholt, W. H., "A Decade Later: Hong Kong's Economy Since 1997," *Hong Kong Journal*, July 2007.

People's Daily (in Chinese), May 13, 2004.

Rajagopalan, N., and Y. Zhang, "Corporate Governance Reforms in China and India: Challenges and Opportunities," *Business Horizon*, Vol. 51, 2008, pp. 55–64.

Rajan, R. G., and L. Zingales, "Financial Dependence and Growth," *American Economic Review*, Vol. 88, 1998, pp. 559–586.

Schipani, C. A., and J. Liu, "Corporate Governance in China: Then and Now," Ann Arbor, Mich.: University of Michigan, Davidson Institute Working Paper Series, 2001.

SEC—*See* U.S. Securities and Exchange Commission.

Shanghai Securities News, December 5, 2006a.

Shanghai Securities News (in Chinese), December 20, 2006b. As of October 7, 2008:
http://web5.jrj.com.cn/news/2006-12-30/000001892140.html

Shi, L., "The Policy Deviation in China's New Media: A Comparative Content Analysis," paper presented at the meeting of the International Communication Association, San Diego, Calif., May 23–27, 2003.

Shleifer, A., and R. Vishny, "A Survey of Corporate Governance," *Journal of Finance*, Vol. 52, No. 2, 1997, pp. 737–783.

Skousen, K. F., S. M. Glover, and D. F. Prawitt, *An Introduction to Corporate Governance and the SEC*, Mason, Ohio: Thomson South-Western, 2005.

Sun, L., and D. Tobin, "International Listing as a Mechanism of Commitment to More Credible Corporate Governance Practices: The Case of the Bank of China (Hong Kong)," *Corporate Governance*, Vol. 13, No. 1, 2005, pp. 81–91.

Supreme People's Court of China, "Announcement on the Temporary Suspending Accepting Cases on Civil Compensation Related to Securities," September 2001.

———, "Announcement on Accepting Civil Infringement Cases Resulting from False Disclosure in the Securities Market," January 2002.

Tam, O. K., "Ethical Issues in Evolution of Corporate Governance in China," *Journal of Business Ethics*, Vol. 37, No. 3, 2002, pp. 303–320.

Tang, S. N., "Bringing in Qualified Strategic Investors and Achieving Mutual Benefits for Chinese and Foreign Banks," speech given at the China Forum (in Chinese), 2005. As of October 6, 2008:
http://art.people.com.cn/GB/41385/70860/4836317.html

Tenev, S., and C. Zhang, *Corporate Governance and Enterprise Reform in China*, Washington, D.C.: World Bank and the International Finance Corporation, 2002.

Tirole, J., "Corporate Governance," *Econometrica*, Vol. 69, No. 1, 2001, pp. 1–35.

Tomasic, R., and N. Andrews, "Minority Shareholder Protection in China's Top 100 Listed Companies," paper presented at the meeting of the Association for Chinese Economic Studies, Melbourne, Australia, July 13–14, 2006.

U.S. Securities and Exchange Commission, *2006 Performance and Accountability Report*, Washington, D.C., 2006a. As of October 6, 2008:
http://www.sec.gov/about/secpar/secpar2006.pdf

———, "SEC and CSRC Announce Terms of Reference for Enhanced Dialogue," press release, May 2, 2006b. As of October 7, 2008:
http://www.sec.gov/news/press/2006/2006-63.htm

Wang, B. S., and Q. Z. Cui, *Principles on China's Company Law*, Beijing, China: China Social Sciences Academic Press, 2006.

Wang, C. F., et al., "Insider Trading and the Regulation on China's Stock Market: International Experience and China's Response," *Guoji Jingrong Yanjiu [Research on International Finance]*, Vol. 3, 2003.

Wang, J., "Dancing with Wolves: Regulation and Deregulation of Foreign Investment in China's Stock Market," *Asian-Pacific Law and Policy Journal*, Vol. 5, 2004, p. 61.

Wang, P. F., and W. C. Duan, "A Study on Performance-Based Incentive Mechanism for State-Owned Enterprises Managers," *Journal of Kunming University of Science and Technology* (in Chinese), Vol. 6, No. 1, 2006, pp. 65–68.

Watts, J., "In China's Richest Village, Peasants Are All Shareholders Now—by Order of the Party," *The Guardian*, May 10, 2005.

Wei, Y., "Baosteel Shares: The Financing Plan Destroys Investor Confidence," *Shanghai Financial News*, August 19, 2004.

Wind Data, homepage, 2007. As of October 22, 2008:
http://www.wind.com.cn/en/home.html

World Bank, *China's Management of Enterprise Assets: The State as Shareholder*, Washington, D.C., Report No. 1, 6265-CHA, 1997.

World Federation of Exchanges, *Annual Report and Statistics of 2006*, 2007.

Wu, G., and M. Tang, "The Civil Liability of Insider Trading," *Dangdai Faxue [Modern Law Science]*, Vol. 150, 2003, pp. 89–92.

Wu, J. L., *Modern Companies and Enterprise Reform*, Tianjin, China: People Press, 1994.

"Wu Jing Lian Nu Chi Gu Shi Hei Zhuang" [Wu Jing Lian Denouncing Market Manipulation], *Economy 30 Minutes*, January 14, 2001. As of October 22, 2008:
http://finance.sina.com.cn/t/32603.html

Wu, X., and P. Xie, 1997, *Debt Consolidation in China's State-Owned Economy*, Beijing, China: China Financial Publishing House, 1997.

Wurgler, J., "Financial Markets and the Allocation of Capital," *Journal of Financial Economics*, Vol. 58, 2000, pp. 187–214.

Xiao, J. Z., Y. K. Zhang, and Z. H. Xie, "The Making of Independent Auditing Standards in China," *Accounting Horizons*, Vol. 14, No. 1, 2000, pp. 69–89.

Xie, G. Z., "Capital Bubble Might Burst but Have Limited Impact upon the Economy," *Southern Metropolitan News*, November 5, 2007.

Xinhua, "Establish Multi-Layered Capital Markets; OTC Market Settled in TBNA" (in Chinese), March 24, 2008. As of October 22, 2008:
http://news.xinhuanet.com/finance/2008-03/24/content_7848535.htm

Yin, G., and F. Wu, "2006 Top Ten CSR (Corporate Social Responsibility) Events in China," *WTO Tribune* (in Chinese), January 21, 2007. As of October 6, 2008:
http://www.csr-china.org/Html/2006chinacsrtopten/071414182696728071510242075227773.html

Yu, "My Suspicion Confirmed," *Zhiquan Shibao [Security Times]*, December 12, 2004. As of October 6, 2008:
http://biz.163.com/41221/9/1848F3UM00020QEU.html

Yuan, J. T., and W. Zhang, "Understanding State Enterprise Reform from a Firm Theory Perspective: Past Experiences and Future Study Directions," *Journal of Guangxi University [Philosophy and Social Science]*, Vol. 25, No. 5, 2003.

Zhang, W. X., "Who Did PetroChina's Four Big Black Candlesticks Lasso? One Hundred Billion Yuan of Wealth Is Weeping," *Li Cai Zhou Bao [21st Century Business Herald]*, November 12, 2007.

Zhang, W. Y., "The Effect, Problem and Solution of China SOEs Reform: A Corporate Governance Perspective," *Social Science Front*, Vol. 2, 1997, pp. 42–51.

———, "China's SOE Reform: A Corporate Governance Perspective," Guanghua School of Management, Peking University, working paper, 1998.

Zheng, Luo, L. N., "The Board of Supervisors: A Dilemmatic Straw Man," *Tongji Yu Juece [Statistics and Decisions]*, Vol. 159, 2003.

Zhong, Z. Y., "Shenzhen Stock Exchange: Far Away from Nasdaq?" *Capital Markets Magazine* (in Chinese), Vol. 5, 2006, pp. 36–42.

Zhou, K. J., "With PetroChina's Allegedly Predatory Buyback, No One Protects Minority Investors," *Beijing Xiandai Shangbao [Beijing Business],* November 2, 2005.

"Zui Gao Fa Yuan: Zan Bu Shou Li Zheng Quan Min Shi Pei Chang An You Dao Li" [The Supreme Court: It Makes Sense Not to Accept Civil Compensation Cases Related to Securities for Now], *Economy 30 Minutes*, October 11, 2001.

Zuo, Z. P., and Y. Gao, "Analysis and Suggestion on the Price Limitation Strategy of Chinese Stock Market," *Journal of Shenyang Institute of Aeronautical Engineering* (in Chinese), Vol. 23, No. 4, 2006, pp. 94–96.